Personal Best

Workbook

B1+ Intermediate

American English

Series Editor
Jim Scrivener

Authors
Elizabeth Walter
and **Kate Woodford**

1	Communication	p2
2	Tell me a story	p8
3	People	p14
4	Places and homes	p20
5	Money and shopping	p26
6	Work and education	p32
7	Entertainment	p38
8	Sports and health	p44
9	Food	p50
10	Right and wrong	p56
11	The natural world	p62
12	Getting away	p68
	WRITING PRACTICE	p74

UNIT 1 Communication

1A LANGUAGE

GRAMMAR: Simple present and continuous; action and state verbs

1 Choose the correct words to complete the sentences. Then write A for action verbs and S for state verbs.

1 Look, that's Hugo! *He's coming / He comes* over to see us. _____
2 Should we open the window? *It's feeling / It feels* hot in here. _____
3 I think we should get a bigger TV and Tom *is agreeing / agrees* with me. _____
4 How often *are they going / do they go* to the gym? _____
5 It's great to see you! *Are you having / Do you have* a good time? _____
6 Anna needs some help. *She's not understanding / doesn't understand* what to do. _____
7 My brother *is working / works* in the U.S. at the moment. _____
8 I'm sure that jacket *is belonging / belongs* to Marcia. _____

2 Complete the sentences with the simple present or present continuous form of the verbs in the box. Use two verbs twice.

| have go make think exist hate |

1 Hannah believes that ghosts really _____.
2 I didn't have time to cook, so we _____ takeout pizza.
3 We _____ to the supermarket once a week.
4 You look happy! What _____ you _____ about?
5 Marco _____ cooking for other people.
6 My sister _____ that I should call our parents more often.
7 _____ you _____ a large apartment?
8 The children _____ a lot of noise because they are very excited.

VOCABULARY: Communication

3 Match the two parts of the sentences.

1 It's very rude to check _____
2 Luckily, he was able to access _____
3 Over 100 people commented _____
4 Michael still keeps _____
5 The couple shared _____
6 I asked Monika to give _____
7 A lot of people go _____
8 When I get _____

a on Suki's latest post.
b in touch with a lot of friends from home.
c me a call later.
d a text message, my phone makes a loud noise.
e online to get medical advice.
f the Internet from his hotel room.
g some of their photographs on social media.
h your phone during dinner with friends.

4 Complete the text with the correct words.

You never see Ethan without his smartphone. He ¹g_____ about 80 text messages a day, and he likes to ²r_____ to them immediately. If you try to ³s_____ to him face-to-face, it can be really annoying because he's always checking his ⁴p_____! He uses Facebook to keep in ⁵t_____ with his friends, and he ⁶c_____ it regularly. He ⁷s_____ lots of photos on it and often ⁸c_____ on his friends' posts. Ethan's parents live in a rural area where it's difficult to ⁹a_____ the Internet, so they don't see his Facebook posts. However, he does ¹⁰g_____ them a call twice a week.

PRONUNCIATION: Sentence stress

5 ▶1.1 Read the sentences. Underline the auxiliary verbs that should be stressed. Listen, check, and repeat.

1 Flora and James are having a party.
2 Does Karl play the piano?
3 Maria isn't feeling very well today.
4 Sasha and Lucia don't want to play tennis.
5 Fatima is studying physics in college.
6 Brett and Owen aren't staying in the same hotel.
7 Ben doesn't have a ticket for the show.
8 Gavin's parents are in Italy.

SKILLS 1B

READING: Skimming a text

Dealing with online trolls

A It's always best to avoid trolls – both the ugly creatures in fairy stories and the equally ugly (on the inside at least) kind who spread their nasty comments by using a computer keyboard. If you look at the comments section of any online newspaper, you will find the second type at work, leaving shocking and unpleasant messages on all sorts of subjects.

B As a society, we value free speech, and, of course, there's a thin line between strong disagreement and messages that are completely unacceptable. But, basically, if someone's main goal is to spread hate and lies, to upset or embarrass someone, or even to scare the person, that person is a troll. Unfortunately, if you use social media, you are sure to have personal experience of trolling sooner or later. Trolls need victims, and they will find them in any online space where people communicate in public.

C If (or when) you meet one, remember that the ability to make you react is like food to a troll – so don't feed them! Trolls are not sensible people. They don't actually want a reasonable discussion, so there's no point at all in trying to have one. It may be tempting to insult or threaten trolls, but they will like this – it is "playing their game," and they are more likely to continue with it than stop. They are only trying to upset you, and if you don't give them a response, they have failed.

D Always remember that the troll is the one with the problem, not you. It's obvious that nobody who hides behind a keyboard to write things he or she would never dare say face-to-face can be a happy and secure person. In fact, newspaper reports of people who have been taken to court for threatening or inappropriate trolling almost always seem to describe sad and lonely lives. Trolls make us furious, but sympathy would probably be a more appropriate emotion.

1 Read the title and look at the pictures. What do you think the article will be about?

 a People who post unpleasant messages online.
 b What to do if your computer is broken.
 c Workers who spend most of their time at a computer.

2 Read the first sentence of each paragraph. Which of A–D do you think will make these points?

 1 It's usually best not to reply to trolls. ____
 2 We should probably feel sorry for trolls. ____
 3 You should try not to have contact with trolls. ____
 4 It can sometimes be difficult to decide if someone is actually a troll. ____

3 Read the sentences. Write T for true sentences, F for false sentences, and D when the article doesn't give you enough information to be sure.

 1 The word "troll" has more than one meaning. ____
 2 Most comments on online newspapers are written by trolls. ____
 3 People can sometimes seem rude when they express strong opinions. ____
 4 It is possible to use social media sites without seeing messages from trolls. ____
 5 Only very intelligent people become trolls. ____
 6 Trolls don't like it if you post angry replies. ____
 7 Trolls always make a great effort to keep their names secret. ____
 8 Trolls are often unhappy people. ____

4 Complete the sentences with your own ideas.

 1 I thought Maria was a vegetarian, but, actually,
 _____.

 2 Philippe told everyone he was a pilot, when he was actually
 _____.

 3 Sara's house doesn't have four bedrooms. In fact,
 _____.

 4 I thought polar bears lived in the Antarctic, but, in fact, they
 _____.

 5 I didn't expect Raj to have many Twitter followers, but, in fact,
 _____.

 6 The doctors thought she had the flu, but, actually,
 _____.

1C LANGUAGE

GRAMMAR: Question forms

1 Complete the questions with the words in the box.

| Is | Did | Does | What | Have | Were |
| Who | How long | Do | Why | | |

1. _____ you have a good time yesterday evening?
2. _____ did the meeting go on for in the end?
3. _____ should we have for dinner tonight?
4. _____ the city of Tijuana in Mexico or the U.S.?
5. _____ you spoken to Peter at all today?
6. _____ did Liam decide to become a vegetarian?
7. _____ your brother have a job?
8. _____ Alice and Ben pleased when you told them the news?
9. _____ were you talking to when I saw you this morning?
10. _____ you know where the castle is?

2 Complete the questions. Use verbs from the answers in the correct form.

1. A _____ her motorcycle?
   B She keeps her motorcycle in the garage.
2. A _____ you for your birthday?
   B He gave me a book.
3. A _____ the guitar?
   B No, Henry can't play the guitar.
4. A _____ her latest movie yet?
   B Yes, I saw it last week.
5. A _____ the concert?
   B Yes, I really enjoyed it.
6. A _____ this letter from my bank? It was private.
   B I opened it, sorry, I thought it was for me.
7. A _____ Ursula?
   B I met her in 2014.
8. A _____ at everyone?
   B Paul was yelling because they weren't listening.
9. A _____ you to write that essay?
   B It took me three days to write it.
10. A _____ all that noise last night? I couldn't sleep.
    B It was the neighbor's cats. I think they were fighting.

VOCABULARY: say, tell, speak, and talk

3 Complete the phrases with say, tell, speak, or talk.

1. _____ German
2. _____ goodbye
3. _____ jokes
4. _____ more slowly
5. _____ you're sorry
6. _____ someone a story
7. _____ to someone about a problem
8. _____ the truth
9. _____ that you are hungry
10. _____ thank you
11. _____ someone a secret
12. _____ nice things to someone

4 Complete the sentences with the past simple of say, tell, or speak.

1. Barbara _____ us that she wanted to be alone.
2. I wonder what Pat _____ to Karl to make him so angry?
3. Orla _____ hello and sat down.
4. The man _____ so quietly that nobody could hear him.
5. Michel _____ us a lie, and now we're not friends.
6. Pilar usually _____ English at school and Spanish at home.
7. I'm sure that Matt _____ the police officer the truth.
8. Louis' boss _____ to him about his performance at work.
9. Who _____ congratulations on passing your exams?
10. Leon _____ that the concert is on Saturday night.

PRONUNCIATION: Question intonation

5 ▶1.2 Read the questions. Write (U) if the intonation should go up or (D) for down. Listen, check, and repeat.

1. Do you like cheese? _____
2. Is Gavin coming to the meeting? _____
3. How many brothers and sisters do you have? _____
4. Why is it so dark in here? _____
5. Is this your jacket? _____
6. Where do you come from? _____
7. Which color do you prefer? _____
8. Can you ride a horse? _____

SKILLS 1D

SPEAKING: Making small talk

1 ▶1.3 Rudy, Bella, and Carina meet at a party. Listen to their conversation. Check (✓) the phrases you hear.

1 Is anyone sitting here? _____
2 I don't think we know each other. _____
3 The food's delicious, isn't it? _____
4 I'm a friend of Cristina's. _____
5 Are you from around here? _____
6 So, what do you do for a living? _____
7 And what does that involve? _____
8 Are you having a good time? _____
9 I love your shirt. Is it new? _____
10 Great to meet you. _____
11 Nice talking to you. _____
12 Have a great evening. _____

2 Look at the phrases you checked in exercise 1. Write S if they are used to start a conversation, A if they are used for asking about a person or situation, and E if they are used to end a conversation.

3 ▶1.3 Rudy, Bella, and Carina often give extra information when they answer questions. For each question, identify the main answer and the extra information from a–j. Listen again if you need to.

1 Have you been dancing? Main _____ Extra _____
2 Are you from around here? Main _____ Extra _____
3 So, what do you do for a living? Main _____ Extra _____
4 And what does that involve? Main _____ Extra _____
5 Are you having a good time? Main _____ Extra _____

a Unfortunately, though, I have to be at work at six tomorrow morning, so I need to leave in a minute.
b But I moved back to Quebec.
c Well, I work with people to help them get in shape.
d Yes, I am.
e I love this music.
f I'm a personal trainer.
g I have clients of all ages, from eighteen to 80!
h No, I used to live here.
i I've been doing it for about three years now.
j Yes, for hours!

4 Complete these conversations with your own ideas. Add an extra piece of information to the answer, and then add a positive comment, as in the example.

1 A Are you having a good day?
  B Yes, thanks. *I played tennis this morning, and I won.*
  A *Oh, great! I'd love to play a game with you some time.*

2 A I like your phone. Is it new?
  B Yes, it is. _____.
  A _____.

3 A Do you enjoy classical music?
  B Not really, to be honest.
  _____.
  A _____.

4 A Where do you work?
  B I work downtown.
  _____.
  A _____.

5

1 REVIEW and PRACTICE

HOME   BLOG   **PODCASTS**   ABOUT   CONTACT

Tom and Sam talk about writing letters.

LISTENING

1 ▶1.4 Listen to the podcast and choose the best words to complete the sentences.

1 Sophie thinks that we should all *communicate more / write more letters / use social media less*.

2 Sophie believes that writing letters can help people *feel less stressed out / go online less / keep in touch with their family*.

2 ▶1.4 Listen again and choose the correct options.

1 Sam asks Tom when he last wrote a letter. What does Tom reply?
   a He can't remember.
   b It was when he was about six.
   c It was about six years ago.

2 How does Sam mainly communicate with her friends?
   a with her phone
   b online
   c with her phone and online

3 According to Sophie, how many teenagers write letters these days?
   a eighteen percent
   b ten percent
   c fourteen percent

4 Tom is surprised that
   a so many young people currently write letters.
   b no young people currently write letters.
   c so few young people currently write letters.

5 Sophie says that when people write to their friends they tell them
   a what has happened in their lives recently.
   b what they think about things.
   c what has happened in their lives and what they think about things.

6 At the end of the interview, Sam says she now wants
   a to write a letter.
   b to receive a letter.
   c someone to write to.

READING

1 Read Penny's blog on page 7 and choose the best summary of her personal challenge last month.

a to watch what people do when they speak
b to improve the way she speaks to people
c to pay more attention to what people tell her

2 Write T for true sentences, F for false sentences, and DS when the writer doesn't say.

1 Penny often blogs about challenges that she has given herself for a month. _____

2 These challenges often involve the person she shares her apartment with. _____

3 Penny is not satisfied with her ability to communicate with other people. _____

4 Penny's roommate knew about Penny's challenge for last month. _____

5 Penny thinks Taylor should try the first point in her plan. _____

6 She made an effort to look at different parts of the speaker's face. _____

7 She says that in our conversations, we should sometimes consider speaking *less*. _____

8 She found it difficult not to look at her phone during the conversations. _____

9 Penny and Taylor had problems in their relationship before Penny started this challenge. _____

10 Taylor noticed their relationship had improved. _____

3 Find seven examples of the verb *tell* in the text.

HOME   BLOG   PODCASTS   ABOUT   CONTACT

Guest blogger Penny tells us how to be a good communicator.

LISTEN AND LEARN!

If you're a regular reader of this blog, you'll be familiar with my 30-day challenges. You'll also know that, although I don't always succeed in these personal challenges, I like to think I learn something along the way. (And you'll probably also know that I have a very patient roommate here – hi, Taylor!)

So are you a good communicator? I like to think I am. I have a wide vocabulary, and I know how to speak to people. What I'm less confident about is my ability to *listen*. So last month's challenge – you guessed it – was to become a better listener. For the last 30 days, when speaking to someone face-to-face, I've followed this four-point plan:

1 Pay attention. Pretend you're going to tell someone else about this conversation in an hour. (This *really* makes you concentrate!)

2 Maintain eye contact. (But don't do this *all* the time – it makes people anxious.)

3 Don't interrupt. (This is a *really* tough one!)

4 Do not check your phone. (Sounds obvious when you read it, right?)

Oh, and in case anyone is wondering, I didn't tell my roommate Taylor at the beginning of the month about my plan to become a better listener. However, I *did* tell her yesterday when I'd finished my challenge. So here's what I learned:

Number 1 *really* works. Honestly – try it! I could probably *still* tell you the details of a conversation I had with Taylor at the start of the month. (Don't worry, Taylor – I'm not telling anyone your secrets here!) This, more than anything, improved my listening skills.

Number 2 is interesting. The idea is to show a polite level of interest by *looking* at the other person when he or she is talking, but not *all the time*. (That would be like an interrogation!) I tried the triangle technique – five seconds looking at each eye, then five seconds at the mouth. It feels strange to begin with, but it allows you to show interest with your eyes without making the other person feel too uncomfortable.

Number 3 is the hardest. The problem is that we *want* to share similar experiences – it's natural. When friends tell us a story about something that happened to them, we want to tell them about a similar thing that happened to us. But sometimes it's better if we just *listen*.

Number 4 wasn't so hard. It's just a bad habit really, and it's impossible to do two things at once!

And did Taylor notice anything different about our conversations? Well, no, she didn't, actually. But, interestingly, she *did* say that she thought we'd gotten along really well recently.

UNIT 2

Tell me a story

2A LANGUAGE

GRAMMAR: Narrative tenses

1 Choose the correct options to complete the sentences.

1. By the time the doctor _____, Freddie was already feeling better.
   a came   b was coming   c comes
2. When I looked in my bag, I realized that my passport _____.
   a disappeared   b was disappearing   c had disappeared
3. We prepared the meal together. I cooked the fish, and Tom _____ a salad.
   a made   b was making   c had made
4. When the man _____ her of lying, she became very angry.
   a accused   b was accusing   c has accused
5. Martha _____ earlier, so we called her to tell her the news.
   a left   b was leaving   c has left
6. Jon and Katie met while they _____ in India.
   a were   b were being   c had been
7. Ollie didn't want to leave the party because he _____ such a great time.
   a had   b was having   c had had
8. I _____ Vera the previous day, so I knew she was in London.
   a saw   b was seeing   c have seen

2 Use the prompts to write sentences with the correct past tenses.

1. Paul/live in Rome/when we meet.
   _____
2. She/not know that/I/guess the truth.
   _____
3. When Colette/show Ben/the photograph/he be/amazed.
   _____
4. Georgia/eat dinner/when Lucy/arrive.
   _____
5. We/get there/at seven but/the others/already go.
   _____
6. They/take/all their furniture so/the room/look very empty.
   _____
7. While Toby/drive to New York/he have/an accident.
   _____

VOCABULARY: -ed and -ing adjectives

3 Match the two parts of the sentences.

1. I hated reading my poems to the class. ____
2. We told the children that we were going to the circus. ____
3. I crashed my parents' car. ____
4. The birds kept trying to steal our food. ____
5. Their boss caught them kissing in the office. ____
6. My grandfather's letters described his adventures in China. ____
7. The rides at the theme park were great. ____
8. Sara and David spent hours visiting the museum. ____

a They were really excited.
b They were extremely annoyed!
c They were absolutely fascinating.
d They were extremely annoying.
e They were so embarrassing!
f They were absolutely fascinated.
g They were really exciting.
h They were so embarrassed!

4 Complete the sentences with -ed or -ing adjectives formed from the verbs in the box.

| terrify | annoy | amuse | fascinate | embarrass | excite |
| amaze | shock | depress | disappoint | | |

1. Rhona's talk was _____ – she made us all laugh.
2. Patrick became _____ after he lost his job.
3. Our plane hit a bad storm – it was absolutely _____.
4. I was _____ to discover that my wallet was missing.
5. It's only a small present – I hope you won't be _____.
6. I want to thank my _____ family for their support.
7. Dan is _____ by animals and often visits the zoo.
8. I hardly slept because of an _____ noise.
9. I couldn't remember his name, which was a bit _____.
10. Florian is very _____ about his trip next month.

PRONUNCIATION: /d/ in the past perfect

5 ▶ 2.1 Listen to the sentences. Write 'd if the past perfect is used.

1. I _____ asked Paul to call a taxi.
2. They _____ cooked us a wonderful meal.
3. She _____ thought he was a very interesting man.
4. We _____ worked together in the past.
5. Unfortunately, he _____ heard every word.
6. He _____ tried to give us some advice.

SKILLS 2B

LISTENING: Listening for the main idea

1 ▶2.2 Listen to a conversation between Anna and her friend Enrico. What is the main idea of their conversation?

a Doing things to bring yourself good luck never works.

b Many people do strange things to try to make themselves lucky, and they sometimes work.

c It is important for athletes to do particular things to give themselves luck.

2 ▶2.2 Listen again. Are the following statements true (T) or false (F)?

1 Anna is surprised that Enrico is wearing a yellow tie. _____

2 Enrico wears the yellow tie every day. _____

3 Anna believes the tie will help Enrico pass his driving test. _____

4 Enrico is certain that he wouldn't be successful without his lucky tie. _____

5 Anna's brother's soccer team does not always win when he eats his lucky banana. _____

6 Michael Jordan thought it was lucky to wear the same shorts he wore on his college team. _____

7 Serena Williams never changes her socks. _____

8 Although he is wearing his lucky tie, Enrico is worried about his driving test. _____

3 ▶2.2 Listen to the conversation again. Complete the phrases that the speakers use to talk about doing something in order to be lucky.

1 ... you think that thing's going to _____ a _____?

2 ... this tie always _____ me _____.

3 It's already _____ me _____ my English exam ...

4 ... having a good luck charm really does _____ people _____.

5 I suppose it's because it _____ them _____.

6 ... he thought it _____ his team _____.

7 Does your lucky tie _____ you from getting _____?

4 ▶2.3 Look at these sentences from Anna and Enrico's conversation. Use the mark _ to show where the consonant-vowel links are. Some sentences have more than one link. Listen, check, and repeat.

1 I'm taking my driving test this afternoon.

2 And you think that thing's going to make a difference?

3 I know you like making fun of me.

4 It's already helped me pass my English exam.

5 My brother always eats what he calls his "lucky banana."

6 Athletes seem to do that sort of thing a lot.

7 Does she wash them after each game?

8 It's clearly not just me who has these strange ideas.

5 Complete the sentences with the correct form of the verbs in the box. There are four extra verbs.

| break | sign | pay | look | set | bring |
| go | try | end | hurry | fall | catch |

1 I went to my hometown for the weekend. It was great to _____ up with old friends.

2 We _____ off early on a long drive in order to catch the eight o'clock flight.

3 I had to stop driving because the cost of gas kept _____ up.

4 Harry and Emma went out for three years, but they _____ up when she went abroad to work.

5 Gemma was the nurse who looked after me when I broke my leg, and we _____ up getting married to each other!

6 Don't lend any more money to Jade – you know she'll never _____ you back.

7 We'll miss the train if you don't _____ up!

8 We were in the clothing store for hours. Grace _____ on at least ten dresses!

2C LANGUAGE

GRAMMAR: *used to* and *usually*

1 Complete the sentences with *used to*, *use to*, or *usually*.

1. When Joe was younger, he _____ go to a country school.
2. Our family didn't _____ have a car.
3. My father _____ came home from work at six.
4. The horses _____ slept in their stable at night.
5. Grandma _____ get angry if we were late for dinner.
6. Did Joe _____ live in the U.S.?
7. Hamida didn't _____ be so adventurous.
8. Did Miriam _____ have long hair?
9. Our family _____ went to Italy in summer.
10. My parents _____ grow all their own vegetables years ago.

2 Complete the sentences with the correct form of the verbs in the box. Use *used to* where possible.

| be | let | help | meet | not have | not get |
| watch | go | babysit | not like | | |

1. When I was younger, I _____ to the movies at least once a week.
2. _____ Gina _____ on the same hockey team as you?
3. Luiza _____ Petar three years ago, I think.
4. Laura's family _____ a television.
5. I _____ cheese, but I absolutely love it now!
6. We always _____ my brother with his homework.
7. Arjun _____ the game on TV last night.
8. _____ your parents _____ you stay out late when you were a teenager?
9. Henry often _____ for his little sister.
10. Andrew and Lottie _____ any exercise at all.

3 Complete the conversation with *usually* or the correct form of *used to* and the verbs in parentheses. Some items have two answers.

A This is the house where we ¹_____ (live) when I was little. I ²_____ (share) a bedroom with both of my sisters.
B Wow, three of you in one room!
A Yes. People ³_____ (not live) in such small houses nowadays, do they? But my parents didn't mind. My mom ⁴_____ (say) that more rooms just meant more housework for her to do!
B That's one way to look at it, I suppose! But I think people ⁵_____ (prefer) bigger houses because they're more comfortable, don't you?
A ⁶_____ (share) a room with your brothers?
B Yes, I did. Mom ⁷_____ (get) really annoyed with us because we stayed up so late, talking and laughing. And then we ⁸_____ (fall) asleep in class and get into trouble!
A You were lucky! My sisters ⁹_____ (not talk) to me very much – they were much older than me. But I ¹⁰_____ (not mind), though. I was happy reading my books.

PRONUNCIATION: Sentence stress

4 ▶ 2.4 Read the sentences and underline the syllables you think will be stressed. Listen and check.

1. I used to love her visits.
2. Did Rod use to play with you?
3. We didn't use to watch TV.
4. Did Katie use to help you?
5. Megan didn't use to come with us.
6. The teachers used to yell a lot.
7. Zoe used to play the piano.
8. Lucas didn't use to ride a bike.
9. Did your teacher use to be late a lot?
10. Maria didn't use to like swimming.

SKILLS 2D

WRITING: Making a narrative interesting

COINCIDENCE IN CAIRO

I had become fascinated with Egypt <u>after</u> spending hours in the Egyptian section of our local museum. As a child, I always wanted to go there. However, my parents weren't thrilled with the idea, so I had to wait <u>until</u> I could afford to pay for the trip myself.

To be honest, I'd almost forgotten about it, but then my friend Angela mentioned that her sister was working in Egypt. ¹_____ So last summer I decided to go there on vacation. I bought a plane ticket from Chicago to Cairo and reserved a hotel downtown that Angela had recommended.

<u>As soon as</u> I arrived, I went straight to the tourist office and reserved a place on a tour of the great Pyramids. ²_____ I turned to look at the person next to me, to see if he or she was as amazed as I was, and, to my surprise, I came face to face with – Angela!

At first I thought Angela was playing a trick on me. "Why didn't you tell me you were coming?" I asked. ³_____

"I'm sorry, do I know you?" she asked, rather suspiciously.
"Come on, Angela!" I said. "What's going on?"
⁴_____ "I don't believe it!" she exclaimed. "People often confuse me with my sister at home, but it's never happened here in Egypt before! Hi, I'm Caroline."

<u>Before</u> I left Cairo, I got together with Caroline a few more times. <u>As soon as</u> I got home, I called Angela. "You told me you had a sister, but you forgot to mention that you were identical twins!" I said.

But still, meeting Caroline in that crowded tourist spot was incredible. ⁵_____

---

1 Read the blog post quickly, ignoring the blanks. Choose the best summary.

 a The narrator went to Egypt, but didn't enjoy his vacation.
 b The narrator went to Egypt and met his friend Angela there.
 c The narrator went on vacation to Egypt and met his friend's sister by chance.

2 Read the blog post again. Match blanks 1–5 with sentences a–g. There are two extra sentences.

 a It was a chance in a million!
 b The sun was high in the clear, blue sky.
 c I was so excited to be there at last, looking at these incredible structures.
 d Then the woman started laughing.
 e She had fair, wavy hair and was wearing a large sun hat.
 f But she just gave me a strange look.
 g That reminded me of my old dream.

3 Look at the underlined words *as soon as*, *before*, *after*, and *until* in the text. Use each word or phrase twice to complete these sentences.

 1 Carlos will need to borrow some money _____ he can buy a car.
 2 _____ I met James, I knew I would marry him.
 3 I spoke to Laurence _____ the show, and he said he had enjoyed it.
 4 Dougal hopes to work as an engineer _____ college.
 5 I'm not hungry, thank you. We ate _____ we went out.
 6 Keir took his exams in June, but he won't get the results _____ August.
 7 Please let me know _____ you have any news about Paul.
 8 Priti had to stay in the office _____ she had finished all her work.

4 Write a blog post about an amazing event. Include two of these sentences in your blog.

 • It was an amazing coincidence!
 • He was tall with long, blond hair and blue eyes.
 • I felt very sad when it was time for us to say goodbye.
 • It was one of the happiest days of my life.
 • Unfortunately, we had missed the last train.
 • It hadn't stopped raining since we arrived.

2 REVIEW and PRACTICE

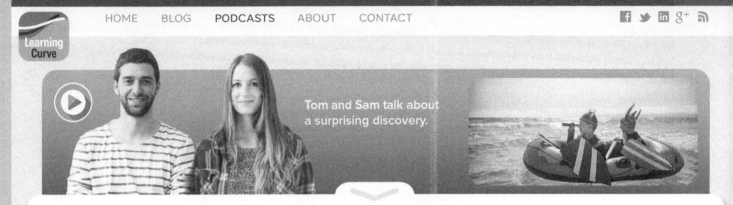

LISTENING

1 ▶ 2.5 Listen to the podcast and choose the best summary of the story.

The man told Tom

a how he had met his wife.

b how he had found his wife in an old photo from when he was a child.

c that he and his wife used to go to the same place on vacation when they were children.

2 ▶ 2.5 Listen again and choose the correct options to complete the sentences.

1 Sam and Tom are wearing similar shoes, but Tom's are
 a made by a different company.
 b much bigger.
 c a different color.

2 The guests on today's show are all describing
 a very surprising things that have happened to them.
 b stories about old photographs.
 c an early get-together with a person who became his or her partner.

3 Adam and Natalie got married
 a while they were in college.
 b a few years after college.
 c just after finishing college.

4 Adam and Natalie discovered that they had
 a been to the same place on vacation.
 b both been to the same school.
 c both been to Mexico.

5 All of the photographs that Adam's mother had brought were
 a from their vacation in California.
 b from their vacations in Mexico.
 c ones in which Adam appeared.

6 Adam was amazed because
 a his brother was in the photograph.
 b he and his brother were on the beach in the photograph.
 c Natalie was in the photograph, too.

READING

1 Read Tom's blog on page 13 and and choose the best summary.

a the different places where Tom has seen celebrities in London

b how easy it is to see celebrities in London

c the experience of seeing a celebrity for the first time

2 Write T for true sentences, F for false sentences, and DS when the writer doesn't say.

1 Tom saw the famous musician in the morning. ____
2 He was late for work when he saw the musician. ____
3 The people near Tom also noticed the musician. ____
4 Tom and the musician spoke to each other. ____
5 This was the first celebrity that Tom had seen. ____
6 Tom's friend is a big fan of James Bond movies. ____
7 Tom thinks that his readers might not believe what his friend told Tom. ____
8 Tom shares his roommate's interest in celebrity vloggers. ____
9 Tom hopes he'll see more celebrities in the future. ____

3 Find six examples of -ed/-ing adjectives in the text.

REVIEW and PRACTICE 2

HOME **BLOG** PODCASTS ABOUT CONTACT

Tom writes about seeing someone famous.

CELEBRITY SPOTTING

Well, that was an exciting way to start the day! There I was at Baker Street station, on my way to work. I was going down the escalator toward the trains when suddenly I saw Adele on the other escalator. She was going up toward the exit. Yes, it really was Adele, the pop star with one of the biggest-selling albums of all time! I was absolutely amazed. If you've had the experience of suddenly seeing a face that you've only ever seen before at the movies or on an album cover you'll know how astonishing this experience is. You can't believe your eyes – you don't think it's really happening. Am I dreaming? What's going on?

Anyway, judging by the excited reaction of the people around me (*Adele, wow! It's Adele! Oh my gosh! I don't believe it!* etc.) I can tell you with absolute certainty that it really was Adele, the singer. And, at last, I was able to proudly tell my friends and family that I'd finally met a famous person. (OK, I didn't exactly meet her...) They say that in London you're never more than a few meters away from a celebrity, but before this morning (and after six whole years in this city), I hadn't laid eyes on a single actor or musician. Very disappointing – oh, wait a minute, I once saw the depressed shopkeeper from a daytime soap opera. Does that count? It does? OK, I'd seen exactly one actor in my six years here! And I can't even remember his name!

Meanwhile, my friend Claire, who lives in a tiny little village outside Oxford, seems to see a famous actor most weeks. For example, if I remember correctly, in the last ten years, she's spotted no less than *three* James Bonds, past and present, in and around Oxford. (As I write that, I realize that you might think that my friend has a rather vivid imagination.) And my roommate here in London sees a celebrity most weeks. Though, when I say "celebrity," of course, we all have different ideas about what a celebrity is. Those of you who know my roommate are aware that he is a *very* enthusiastic follower of five or six "celebrity vloggers." Now, I don't even know the names of these "celebrities" and I'm pretty sure that I could walk past *any* of them in the street without recognizing them.

Still, now I've spotted one of the biggest celebrities on the planet – perhaps she'll be the first of many?

UNIT 3 People

3A LANGUAGE

GRAMMAR: Future forms: present continuous, *be going to* and *will*

1 Choose the correct verbs to complete the sentences.

1 "Do you know Rocco's date of birth?" "No, *I'll ask / I'm asking* him later."
2 It's a beautiful day. *Will we go / Should we go* to the beach?
3 What *will you do / are you doing* next weekend?
4 I failed my driving test. *Are you helping / Will you help* me practice?
5 *Are we going to / Will we* invite Sara to their wedding?
6 "I can't do my homework." "*I'm helping / I'll help* you, if you'd like."
7 Max *will come / is coming* back from Australia on Friday.
8 I'm going to a concert tomorrow. *Should I / Am I going to* get you a ticket?

2 Complete the conversations with the present continuous, *going to*, *will*, or *should* and the verb in parentheses. There may be more than one answer.

A ¹_____(visit) anywhere exciting on vacation this year?
B Yes, Kenya. But we ²_____(not travel) with a group.
A I've got a fantastic book about Kenya. I ³_____(lend) it to you.

A The movie you were talking about is on next week. ⁴_____(go) and see it together?
B Great! I ⁵_____(get) tickets later.
A Really? I work closer to the theater than you.
B Don't worry – I ⁶_____(do) it online.

A ⁷_____(make) dinner for you tonight?
B Actually, I ⁸_____(meet) Joe this evening. We ⁹_____(play) tennis and then get pizza.
A OK, I ¹⁰_____(not make) anything for you, then.

VOCABULARY: Personality adjectives

3 Read the sentences and match the people with the adjectives in the box. There are two extra adjectives.

| unsociable | dishonest | insensitive | impolite |
| easygoing | disorganized | confident | impatient |

1 Robert would be very happy to make a speech in front of 1,000 people. _____
2 Kira knows I don't have much money, but she keeps telling me about expensive things she's bought. _____
3 Andrew's always missing meetings because he doesn't write them in his diary. _____
4 On the weekends, Adam's usually happy to do whatever his friends suggest. _____
5 Gloria doesn't like parties – she'd rather stay at home and read a book. _____
6 Chuck hates having to wait for other people – he just wants to get moving with things. _____

4 Complete the personality adjectives.

1 Why did you refuse to speak to Suzie? That was really u_____.
2 Maya has been very h_____ – she's cleaned the bathroom and prepared dinner.
3 Don't ask Helen for a ride if you need to be there on time – she's too u_____.
4 Laurie is feeling a _____ about his exam because he hasn't prepared well enough.
5 Ella always makes the decisions in our house – she's extremely s_____.
6 It's d_____ to tell the customers that the milk is organic when it's not.
7 It was so i_____ of them to talk while the professor was speaking.
8 Everyone at my new school is very f_____, so I didn't feel at all lonely.

PRONUNCIATION: *going to*

5 ▶3.1 Check (✓) the sentences where *going to* can be pronounced /ˈɡʌnə/. Listen and check.

1 Are you going to buy Hamish a present? ___
2 Alice is going to Cleveland next week. ___
3 I think my mom's going to be really angry. ___
4 I'm going to ask my teacher to explain. ___
5 Is Tom going to the concert with you? ___
6 Are we going to have dinner now? ___

14

SKILLS 3B

READING: Reading for specific information

Twin personalities?

A Mark and Ollie are identical twins. They look so alike that when they were little even their mother had to look carefully to see which one she was speaking to, and they certainly used this to play tricks on teachers or friends! Now they are twenty, and although they still look very similar (Mark is slightly larger as he works out at the gym most days), their personalities could hardly be more different.

B "I'm the sociable one," Mark says. "I love meeting new people, trying new activities, traveling, things like that. Ollie's the opposite – it's not that he's unfriendly, but he'd rather stay at home and read a book."

C So how common is it for twins to have such different personalities? Well, psychologists used to think that twins developed pretty much independently, each one shaped by his or her own life experiences. So they would have thought that Mark and Ollie were typical. However, recent research has challenged this view.

D Researchers from Edinburgh University studied 800 sets of twins. Focusing on qualities that contribute to success in life (such as self-control and willingness to work hard), they found that twins are twice as likely to share personality traits than other brothers and sisters. Amazingly, a similar study carried out at the University of Minnesota found that twins raised in different families are even more likely to share personality traits. In fact, two subjects of the study, brothers Jim Lewis and Jim Springer, who were brought up separately, were so similar that it was almost impossible to tell them apart.

E Twins Rachel and Annie, who grew up together, aren't surprised that twins raised in the same family end up being more different from each other. "Since we looked so alike, people sometimes treated us as if we were just one person," Annie explains. "And we hated it. That's why we made a deliberate effort to be different. When Rachel started playing soccer, I took up the piano, so she became the athletic one, and I was the creative one."

1 Skim the text quickly. Match paragraphs A–E with summaries 1–5.

1 Ideas about twins and personality have changed over time. ____
2 These two brothers look very similar. ____
3 Research shows that twins naturally have similar personalities. ____
4 Why two sisters want to be different from one another. ____
5 How one man differs from his brother. ____

2 Read the questions and <u>underline</u> the key words. Then choose the correct answers.

1 What could Mark and Ollie do because they looked so similar?
 a make people believe that one of them was the other
 b miss school
 c make their friends laugh
2 How different are Mark and Ollie's personalities?
 a very different
 b slightly different
 c not very different
3 In the past, where did scientists believe most personality traits in twins came from?
 a the personality of their parents
 b things that happened in their lives
 c the way their families treated them
4 What areas of personality did the Edinburgh research study most?
 a all aspects
 b aspects that are likely to be different between twins
 c aspects connected to people's achievements
5 Why did Rachel and Annie deliberately try to be different from each other?
 a They didn't want other people to know who each girl was.
 b It was important for them to have their own identities.
 c They thought it would be boring for them to be the same.

3 Choose the correct words to complete the sentences.

1 The bus broke down. *So / Since / That's why* we're so late.
2 I didn't invite Polly *so / as / that's why* she's not one of my friends.
3 Alex has lost his key, *so / since / that's why* he'll have to break the window to get in.
4 Let's have a cup of tea *since / so / that's why* we're still waiting for Clara to arrive.
5 I know Bella pretty well *that's why / so / as* we work in the same building.
6 Ruth didn't have a towel, *since / so / that's why* she dried herself on an old T-shirt.

3C LANGUAGE

GRAMMAR: Defining and non-defining relative clauses

1 Choose the correct options. Parentheses show that you can omit the pronoun.

1. Gary walked to the station, _____ his friend was waiting.
   a who   b that   c where   d (which)
2. The box, _____ was very heavy, contained more than twenty books.
   a (which)   b which   c (that)   d who
3. He's the man _____ lives in the house across the street.
   a whose   b (who)   c which   d that
4. Is this the car _____ you're thinking of buying?
   a (that)   b where   c whose   d (who)
5. Lucas, _____ parents are in the army, has moved many times.
   a who   b (that)   c whose   d which
6. There will be a prize for the person _____ writes the best story.
   a (who)   b (that)   c whose   d who
7. She's the woman _____ works in the bank.
   a (who)   b that   c where   d (that)
8. Did I show you the photo _____ I took?
   a (that)   b whose   c which   d where

2 Write relative clauses to include the information in parentheses. Add commas where necessary and omit the relative pronouns where possible.

1. Where have you put the bag? (I gave it to you.)
   Where have you put the bag I gave you?
2. My aunt is planning to sail around the world. (She's very adventurous.)
   My aunt _____ is planning to sail around the world.
3. The woman is very upset. (Her dog has run away.)
   The woman _____ is very upset.
4. I've been to the office. (Rupert works there.)
   I've been to the office _____ works.
5. There's the man. (He comes to cut the grass.)
   There's the man _____.
6. I'm going to New York! (It's exciting.)
   I'm going to New York _____ exciting!
7. Is that the boy? (You told me about him.)
   Is that the boy _____ about?

VOCABULARY: Relationships

3 Read the sentences and check (✓) True or False.

		True	False
1	Close friends always live near each other.	True	False
2	Children in the U.S. usually live with their relatives.	True	False
3	It's upsetting to have a falling out with a friend.	True	False
4	Most people would like to get along well with their family.	True	False
5	You can't have classmates if you're not a student.	True	False
6	If people make up, they can never be friends again.	True	False
7	We introduce someone to people they've met before.	True	False
8	Your next-door neighbor lives in the nearest house.	True	False
9	Any two friends can be described as "a couple."	True	False
10	If you have a lot in common with someone, lots of things about your lives are similar.	True	False

4 Complete the text with relationship words.

I moved to Mexico City two years ago to start a new job. At work, my new ¹c_____ were very friendly, but I was still lonely at first. Back at home in Tijuana, I used to hang out with my ²b_____ friend Alejandro most weekends, and I missed him a lot. However, things soon got better. I joined a gym, and I gradually got to ³k_____ people. Now I ⁴g_____ along especially well with a guy called Felipe. In fact, it was Felipe who ⁵i_____ me to my ⁶g_____, Mercedes – we're getting married next year. Mercedes and I have so much in ⁷c_____ – we are both engineers, and we love music. We also have very strong opinions, and we sometimes ⁸a_____ – especially about politics – but we always ⁹m_____ up before too long! Last year, I took Mercedes to Tijuana to meet my ¹⁰p_____ and some of my other ¹¹r_____. They loved her. While we were there, we got ¹²t_____ with all my old friends, too, which was great!

PRONUNCIATION: Pausing in relative clauses

5 ▶3.2 Read the sentences aloud, pausing when there are commas. Listen, check, and repeat.

1. We often eat paella, which is a Spanish dish.
2. Is that the man who lives next door to Sam?
3. My colleagues, who are really friendly, planned a birthday party for me.
4. I get along well with my brother, who is two years older than me.
5. The town where I grew up is very small.
6. This necklace, which belonged to my grandmother, is my favorite.

SKILLS 3D

SPEAKING: Giving and responding to news

1 ▶ 3.3 Listen to the conversation between Lily and her roommate, Anne. Are the following statements true (T) or false (F)?

1 Lily is pleased that Raj is coming. _____
2 Raj called when Lily was not at home. _____
3 Raj forgot to apply for a visa. _____
4 Raj has only been to the UK once before. _____
5 In the end, Raj is allowed to travel to the UK. _____
6 Anne does not want her to become too friendly with Raj. _____

2 ▶ 3.3 Listen again and choose the correct options.

1 How did Anne give Lily some bad news?
  a I'm sorry, but I have something bad to tell you.
  b I'm afraid I have some bad news.
  c I'm really sorry to give you this bad news.
2 How did Lily respond?
  a Oh no, I don't believe it!
  b Oh, that's horrible!
  c Oh no, that's terrible!
3 How did Anne show sympathy?
  a That's terrible!
  b What a shame!
  c It's not fair!
4 How did Anne give Lily some good news?
  a Guess what?
  b Great news!
  c I have some good news for you.
5 How did Lily respond?
  a I'm so happy!
  b That's fantastic news!
  c Oh, that's a relief!
6 How did Anne show that she was pleased, too?
  a I'm so happy for you!
  b I'm absolutely thrilled for you!
  c That's fantastic news!

3 ▶ 3.4 Complete the conversations. Then listen and check.

1 A I have some good n_____! I passed my driving test!
  B C_____! Now you can give me a ride to school!
2 A I'm really s_____ to give you this news, but I can't come to your wedding. I have an important exam that day.
  B Oh, what a s_____! I really wanted you to be there.
3 A Great n_____! The doctor says there's nothing wrong with me.
  B Oh, that's a r_____!
4 A A_____ what? I just got an e-mail saying I've won a major poetry competition.
  B Oh, wow! I'm absolutely t_____ for you!
5 A I'm a_____ I have some bad news. Toby's dog has died.
  B Oh no, that's t_____!

4 Mr. Allsworth (A) is telling his student Cara (B) that her grades aren't good enough to get accepted into a program where she had hoped to study. Read the conversation and complete A with your own words.

A (Say that you have some bad news for her.)
_____

B Oh no, what is it?

A (Explain that she needs at least a grade B to get accepted into the program.)
_____

B Yes, that's right. If I get less than a grade B, they won't accept me.

A (Give her the bad news.)
_____

B Oh no! That means I'll have to take the exam again.

A (Tell her that you're really sorry.)
_____

B Thank you. I guess I'll need to work harder next time.

3 REVIEW and PRACTICE

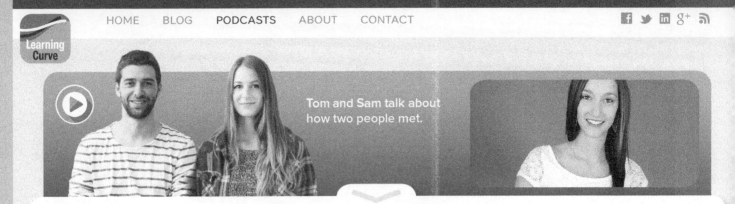

HOME   BLOG   **PODCASTS**   ABOUT   CONTACT

Tom and Sam talk about how two people met.

LISTENING

1 ▶ 3.5 Listen to the podcast and number words a–f in the order you hear them (1–6).

a bathroom ____
b cell phone number ____
c party ____
d vacation ____
e cloth ____
f drink ____

2 ▶ 3.5 Listen again and complete the sentences with one or two words.

1 Daisy and Izzie are now _____.
2 One of Izzie's _____ introduced them at a party.
3 Julia thought they would have a lot _____.
4 Izzie thought that Daisy was _____, but now understands that she is just shy.
5 Daisy thought that Izzie was _____ and _____.
6 Izzie ran off to _____ to find a cloth, but Daisy had disappeared.
7 Daisy went to hide in the bathroom because she felt _____.
8 Izzie didn't realize that Daisy was so _____ because of the accident with Izzie's drink.
9 When they got together again after the party, Daisy _____ to Izzie.
10 Next week, they are traveling to _____ together.

READING

1 Read Sam's blog on page 19 and number points a–e in the order they appear (1–5).

a Best friends who are different are more likely to help each other. ____
b Best friends find the differences between them interesting. ____
c Friendships are more likely to succeed between people who are very different. ____
d We don't try to be better than friends who are very different from us. ____
e With "opposite friends" we are prepared to try out things we haven't done before. ____

2 Check (✓) the statements that are true.

1 Sam has always had a very strong opinion about this subject. ____
2 The researchers did not study many pairs of friends. ____
3 Romantic relationships generally work better between personalities that are similar. ____
4 Sam is good at finding her way to places. ____
5 There are advantages when one friend provides a skill that the other friend does not have. ____
6 Friends who are similar to us encourage us to try new things. ____
7 Friends who have different qualities from each other are less competitive. ____
8 The perfect friend would be someone who behaves in exactly the same way as you. ____

REVIEW and PRACTICE 3

HOME **BLOG** PODCASTS ABOUT CONTACT

Sam writes about what attracts us to other people.

OPPOSITES ATTRACT!

Have you ever found yourself saying, "Opposites attract!" about a couple that you know, or a friendship in your social circle? I know I have. (I've never been able to decide whether it was true, by the way!) I just read a fascinating article on the subject, and I'm going to share the main points with you. (A bit of background for your information: researchers studied the personalities of over a thousand pairs of best friends.)

So, it turns out we were right about friends. Friendships do work best between people with very different qualities where, for example, best friend A is confident, disorganized, and easygoing, and best friend B is shy, reliable, and anxious. (Interestingly, this is not the case for romantic relationships, where previous studies have shown that opposite personality types are *less likely* to lead to successful, long-term relationships.) There are several reasons for this.

1 The "opposites attract" friends bring different qualities and abilities to the relationship, and this is useful. For example, the person with no sense of direction (that's me!) will probably have a better time when he or she is with a friend who knows exactly how to get to where they're going. The very shy person (er, not me!) will have more success at a party with a sociable friend who can introduce him or her to new people, and so on.

2 Opposites force each other out of their comfort zones. You know how it goes – you feel anxious about doing something new for the first time, but, afterwards, you're really glad that your friend persuaded you to do it. Friends who have the same interests and qualities as us don't challenge us to experience new things. Friends who are very different from us introduce us to new activities and experiences and this, apparently, helps us to "grow" as people.

3 Opposites are free to be themselves. With their different strengths and skills, they're not both trying to be "the organized one," for example, or "the sociable one." Neither friend is competing in the relationship. This results in a happier, less competitive friendship.

4 Opposites don't get bored with each other. Simply, the differences between us keep us interested. This point reminds me that I once read somewhere that it would be people's worst nightmare if they met themselves. (Imagine knowing exactly what the other "you" was thinking and how this other "you" was going to respond to something …)

The next time I find myself getting frustrated because I don't understand why a friend is behaving in a particular way, I'm going to stop and celebrate the differences between us.

UNIT 4 Places and homes

4A LANGUAGE

GRAMMAR: Quantifiers

1 Choose the correct options to complete the sentences.

1 This soup is horrible! I put _____ salt in it.
   a too much   b plenty of   c too many

2 The local people gave us _____ of their traditional food.
   a few   b a little   c much

3 We couldn't buy clothes because we had _____ money.
   a not any   b not enough   c no

4 There wasn't _____ room for us all to get on the bus.
   a lots of   b enough   c plenty

5 There's _____ chance that Hal will win the competition.
   a not much   b not enough   c too much

6 You can't swim today. It's _____ cold!
   a too much   b enough   c too

7 _____ people want ice cream in the winter.
   a Little   b Not much   c Not many

8 We couldn't make a fire because there wasn't _____ wood.
   a plenty   b any   c lots of

2 Read the sentences and write appropriate responses. Use the words in parentheses in the correct form.

1 The bus holds 40 people, and 80 people want to travel.
   The bus _____.
   (is/big)

2 You can bring your whole family to stay.
   We _____
   (plenty/bedrooms)

3 I can't afford to buy this coat.
   It _____
   (too/money)

4 It's hard to buy nice clothes where I live.
   There _____
   in town. (many/stores)

5 The museum is really popular with tourists.
   _____ to visit it. (people/want)

6 Dinner's not ready yet.
   You will have to _____
   (wait/minutes)

7 We can't have omelets for lunch.
   There _____
   (no/eggs)

VOCABULARY: Compound nouns

3 Match the two parts of the sentences.

1 You shouldn't ride your bike _____
2 I bought a pair of pants and some plates _____
3 Harry was late getting home because he was stuck _____
4 Sue drove into town and left her car _____
5 There is a good collection of modern paintings _____
6 We usually play squash on the courts _____

   a in a traffic jam.
   b at the sports center.
   c in a pedestrian area.
   d in a parking lot.
   e at a department store.
   f at the art gallery.

4 Complete the text with compound nouns.

I live just outside the city, but my office is downtown, so I have to commute to work every day. When the weather's good, I ride my bike. Luckily, there is a good ¹_____ path that goes almost all the way to my office. And when it rains, there's an excellent ²_____ transportation system, so I never use my car to get to work – it would be silly to spend time sitting in a traffic ³_____ when there's a bus every ten minutes!
This is a great city for a young person like me to live in. There's a huge ⁴_____ mall – I often go to the sporting-goods stores there on my lunch hour. And the night ⁵_____ is great, too, with plenty of movie theaters, restaurants, and ⁶_____ clubs. There's a big sports ⁷_____ near my apartment, where I play soccer with my friends on the weekends.

PRONUNCIATION: Sentence stress

5 ▶ 4.1 Read the sentences and underline the syllables you think will be stressed. Listen and check.

1 The children made lots of noise.
2 Are there enough sandwiches?
3 We don't have any towels.
4 She gave me too much rice.
5 Make sure there's plenty of water.
6 Let's pick a few strawberries.

SKILLS 4B

LISTENING: Understanding key points

1 ▶ 4.2 Patrizia has gone to see a real estate agent in order to rent an apartment. Listen to their conversation and choose the correct options.

1 Why does Patrizia want to live alone?
   a She is worried that other people won't like her dog.
   b She has had her own place for a long time and does not want to share again.
   c She thinks it's cheaper to live on your own.
2 Why will it be more difficult for her to find an apartment?
   a There aren't many apartments where you can keep a dog.
   b There aren't many luxury apartments available.
   c A lot of apartments are not clean and bright.
3 She says that it's not important to live close to school because
   a having somewhere for her dog is more important.
   b she is willing to travel a pretty long way by bike.
   c she is only going there for one year.
4 Why does she want to live somewhere with lots of restaurants and cafés?
   a She will not have time to cook.
   b Areas like that are more interesting.
   c She doesn't want to cook her own meals.
5 She doesn't want the first apartment the real estate agent suggests because
   a she hates riding in elevators.
   b she doesn't want to live with people who work downtown.
   c she doesn't think she would like the area.
6 Why is the second apartment more suitable for her dog?
   a They will not need to ride in an elevator.
   b The dog likes walking up and down the stairs.
   c It is in a lively area.

2 ▶ 4.3 Listen to the sentences from Patrizia's conversation. Focus on the way they use different words to repeat key points. Complete the sentences.

1 Did you want a place of your own, or are you happy to _____ with other people?.
2 No, I've lived _____ for four years now, and I don't want to live with other people again.
3 Obviously, an apartment just for you will be a little more expensive. It's _____ to share.
4 It's not very interesting around there, is it? I'm worried it could be a bit _____.
5 It's in a much livelier area. I think it would be more _____.

3 ▶ 4.4 Look at the sentences. Use the mark _ to show links between consonants with similar sounds. One sentence has more than one link. Listen, check, and repeat.

1 When do you plan to leave Venice?
2 I have to take Katie to the station.
3 Dan's mom made him stay inside.
4 Polly told me she'd done yoga before.
5 Where did you buy your jacket?
6 I tried to fix Sue's broken laptop.
7 I hope Lara won't feel lonely.
8 Morgan made a really good dessert.

4 Use a different form of the same verb to complete both sentences in 1–8.

1 a I have _____ Kelly for a long time.
   b We will contact you when we _____ more facts about the situation.
2 a We _____ a great time in France last summer.
   b Why don't you _____ something to eat before we set off again?
3 a Unfortunately, Simon's team _____ the game.
   b I gave Mel my address and phone number so that we don't _____ contact.
4 a When I _____ Eva for the first time, I thought she was really scary!
   b Izzie's planning to _____ a friend for coffee this afternoon.
5 a I feel terrible – I think I've _____ Toni's cold.
   b Amit _____ a cab when he misses the last bus.
6 a My sister _____ borrowing my clothes without asking.
   b George said he would come back, and he _____ his promise.
7 a Suzi was late because she _____ her bus.
   b I'm sure you would _____ your brother if he went to live abroad.
8 a Is it OK to _____ photos in here?
   b The man came into the room and _____ his coat off.

4C LANGUAGE

GRAMMAR: Comparatives and superlatives, as ... as

1 Complete the sentences with the phrases in the box.

> the best of   as good as   less difficult
> the most difficult   by far the best
> the least difficult   one of the best
> as difficult as

1 Louis is _____ soccer player on our team.
2 Clara was _____ pianists I had ever heard.
3 Saying goodbye to my parents was _____ thing I've ever done.
4 After I gave up sugar, losing weight wasn't _____ I thought it would be.
5 Kari is really stressed out. She needs to find a _____ job.
6 Pilar, Rafaelle, and Maya are all good at math, but Maya is _____ the three.
7 Neil's new, so we're giving him _____ work to begin with.
8 I don't think this restaurant is _____ it used to be.

2 Complete the sentences with the adjectives in the box. Add any other words necessary.

> hot   bad   angry   expensive   easy
> late   far   beautiful

1 I failed my French exam but I passed Spanish. I find Spanish far _____ French.
2 It takes me ten minutes to bike home, but it takes Aidan 20 minutes because he lives _____ away than me.
3 We stay inside around lunchtime because it is _____ part of the day.
4 I didn't stay up _____ as my friends because I had to get up early.
5 The Taj Mahal is _____ building I have ever seen.
6 When we tried to apologize, Sara seemed to get even _____.
7 We had very little money, so we bought _____ computer in the store.
8 I thought his last novel was bad, but this one is even _____ than that.

VOCABULARY: Describing homes

3 Choose the correct words to complete the sentences.

1 Sophia has three sofas in her *basic / spacious / cozy* living room.
2 Tom's kitchen is really *old-fashioned / stylish / modern* – he certainly doesn't have a dishwasher!
3 It's a two-minute walk to the supermarket, so that's very *comfortable / convenient / basic*.
4 They have a *bright / convenient / huge* garden that takes up a lot of their time.
5 There's a shower but no bathtub because my bathroom is so *tiny / cozy / old-fashioned*.
6 This room will look more *basic / spacious / cozy* with some rugs.
7 Lou's bedroom only has a closet and a bed, so it's pretty *basic / stylish / bright*.
8 Her kitchen's *stylish / dark / cozy* with that big tree outside.

4 Complete the words.

1 My apartment's on the _____p floor and has a great view.
2 Furniture we didn't use was stored down in the b_____t.
3 I live in the s_____s because it's cheaper than downtown.
4 There is just one shopping m_____ in the small town where I live.
5 Grandma has a f_____ floor apartment without stairs.
6 Does this t_____n have a library and a post office?
7 My bedroom has a b_____y outside that I often sit on.
8 In the summer, do you often eat out on the roof t_____e?
9 Max lives on the sixteenth floor of an a_____t building.
10 They had been to the c_____y, walking among the trees and fields.

PRONUNCIATION: /ə/ sound

5 ▶4.5 Listen to the sentences. Do the underlined words contain the /ə/ sound? Write ✓ or ✗.

1 My sister's <u>not</u> <u>as</u> tall <u>as</u> me. _____ _____ _____
2 Dan is by <u>far</u> <u>the</u> best tennis player I <u>know</u>. _____ _____ _____
3 It's <u>a</u> bit <u>cooler</u> today <u>than</u> yesterday. _____ _____ _____
4 Gabi is <u>better</u> <u>than</u> me at <u>ballet</u>. _____ _____ _____
5 I'd like to get <u>a</u> <u>bigger</u> <u>apartment</u>. _____ _____ _____
6 This is the <u>longest</u> <u>of</u> all <u>the</u> books. _____ _____ _____

SKILLS 4D

WRITING: Writing an informal e-mail

1 Read Owen's e-mail to his friend Gabe. Divide it into six paragraphs by putting a / at the end of each one.

Hey Gabe,

Great to hear from you! Sorry for not writing sooner. Fantastic news about your new job in Los Angeles! I hope you're enjoying it. I hear the nightlife is really good there. Can't wait to come and see you. Do you have your own apartment? Anyway, everything's fine here, except that my sister was in a car crash last week! Luckily, nobody was hurt, but the car's in terrible shape. It's going to cost her a fortune to repair it. So she's riding her bike everywhere at the moment and complaining about it all the time! Speaking of bike riding, did I tell you that Kenny and I are planning to take our bikes to Colorado this summer? There's a great route through the mountains that we want to try. Not sure if Kenny can ride up a mountain, though. ;-) He hasn't trained much recently because he has a new girlfriend, and he's spending all of his time with her. You could come with us, too, if you're free – you're in much better shape than Kenny, after all! By the way, did you hear that the Los Angeles Angels aren't doing too well this year? Not sure if I'll buy a season ticket next year. It's hard to support a team that loses. Anyway, have to go now – need to be at work early tomorrow, so it has to be an early night. Let me know what you think about the Colorado trip.

All the best,

Owen

2 Find the informal sentences in the e-mail that have the same meaning as these more formal sentences (1–6).

1 I am looking forward to visiting you in Los Angeles.
2 I should stop writing now.
3 I apologize for not replying to your e-mail before now.
4 I was very pleased to hear that you have a new job.
5 I have not decided if I should buy a season ticket next year.
6 Thank you very much for your e-mail.

3 Read the pairs of sentences (1–6). Fill in the blanks with the discourse markers in the box. There may be more than one answer.

| So, …   Anyway, …   By the way, …   Speaking of … |

1 … and he's going to be in the hospital for about a month.
_____ I also have some much happier news to give you – I got the job at the restaurant!

2 … I've worked a lot of extra hours recently, so I've had a bit more money, and I've bought myself a really good tent.
_____ camping, do you feel like taking a trip next weekend?

3 … so it's really important that you sign the document.
_____ have you seen Martha recently? I heard that she broke up with Josh.

4 … and I ended up missing my plane – it was such a disaster!
_____ Matt says to tell you that he wants his coat back. He says you borrowed it a month ago.

5 … and we all went out to celebrate because Hayley passed her driving test.
_____ driving tests, when are you taking yours?

6 … I had to borrow a bike from George to get there on time!
_____ what do you think of George's new girlfriend?

4 Imagine you are Gabe. Reply to Owen's e-mail. Write six paragraphs and include some of the informal discourse markers from exercise 3. Use some of these ideas.

- Express sympathy for Owen's sister.
- Talk about your new job and apartment in Los Angeles.
- Invite Owen to stay.
- Accept Owen's invitation to go bicycling in Colorado OR give a reason why you can't go.
- Say something about the Los Angeles Angels or a team you support.

4 REVIEW and PRACTICE

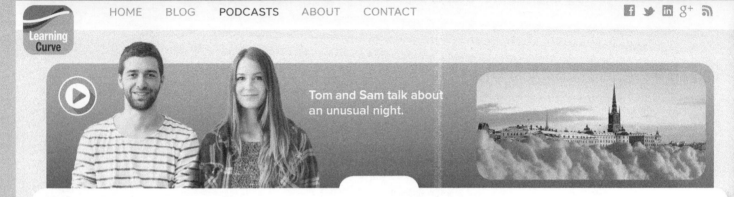

HOME   BLOG   **PODCASTS**   ABOUT   CONTACT

Tom and Sam talk about an unusual night.

LISTENING

1 ▶ 4.6 Listen to the podcast and number a–e in the order in which they happen (1–5).

a Olivia and her daughter got into a cab. _____
b Olivia and her daughter were shopping in a department store. _____
c They found themselves in a terrible traffic jam. _____
d They slept in the department store. _____
e They returned to the department store. _____

2 ▶ 4.6 Listen again and choose the correct options.

1 According to Tom, Sam always sleeps
   a in unusual places.
   b in expensive hotels.
   c on friends' sofas.
2 What caused the problem for Olivia and her daughter?
   a There was heavy snow.
   b There weren't enough cabs.
   c The store closed early.
3 After getting out of the cab, where did they go to?
   a a nearby café
   b a bedding store
   c the same department store
4 While they were waiting for the snow to stop, they
   a looked out of the window.
   b sat on the beds.
   c ate some food.
5 Where did they spend the night?
   a in the basement
   b on the first floor
   c on the second floor
6 How was Olivia and her daughter's night at the department store?
   a rather uncomfortable
   b very comfortable
   c pretty cold

READING

1 Read Simon's blog on page 25 and choose the best summary of Simon's reasons for visiting his friend, Al.

a He wanted to show his friends that he could do new things.
b He wanted to help Al build a hut to sleep in.
c He wanted to find out what it was like to live in the country.

2 According to the blog post, are the sentences true (T), false (F), or the writer doesn't say (DS)?

1 Simon loves cities, but hasn't always lived in one. _____
2 Simon enjoys the nightlife that the city has to offer. _____
3 Simon often uses public transportation where he lives. _____
4 Simon isn't always completely satisfied with city life. _____
5 Al prefers cold showers to hot showers. _____
6 Simon didn't leave Al's field all week. _____
7 Simon did all the cooking while he was staying with Al. _____
8 While Simon was staying with him, Al slept outdoors. _____

3 Find compound nouns in the text to match definitions 1–6.

1 A place where you can get exercise
2 A place where you can buy lots of different things
3 A system of vehicles that anyone can use
4 When cars and other vehicles are in a line and cannot move
5 A place where you can see paintings
6 A place where you go dancing

REVIEW and PRACTICE 4

HOME BLOG PODCASTS ABOUT CONTACT

Guest blogger Simon writes about his visit to the country.

GETTING AWAY FROM IT ALL

As readers of this blog know, at heart I'm a city person, despite growing up on a farm. OK, there are plenty of things about the city that I don't particularly like. For example, you won't find me in a nightclub at three o'clock in the morning, and, as I've said before, I'm no fan of this city's many shopping malls. However, there are certain aspects of city life that I really do appreciate – the art galleries, the theaters, the restaurants and cafés, and so on. And as a non-driver, I find the public transportation you get in a city very convenient.

That said, from time to time I wonder whether there's a better life out there in the country, away from all the traffic jams, the constant noise, and, of course, the pollution. (Doesn't everyone?) So to explore this idea, last week I went to stay with my old high school friend, Al, who lives in a field. Yes, readers, a field! Admittedly, he has a shelter to sleep in – a small, wooden hut that he built himself. But pretty much everything else, such as cooking and washing, for example, he does outdoors. I'm sure Al wouldn't mind me saying this, but as accommodations go, it's *pretty* basic.

Now, I don't know about you, readers, but I take a shower every day, and I like being able to wash my clothes once in a while, so for me, this was a new experience. To start, there was very little hot water. Al, who somehow always manages to look very clean, washes in a solar-powered outdoor shower, but last week, there wasn't enough sun to make the water really warm. Halfway through the week, I considered the shower option, but having tested the temperature with my hand, I decided, instead, to take advantage of the facilities in the local sports center. (I know, I know!)

However, I have to say that, overall, I really enjoyed the experience of living closer to nature. I loved hearing the birds sing as I chopped vegetables for dinner in the outdoor kitchen. Reading my book on what Al calls his "roof terrace" – the very strong (!) roof of his hut, I felt more relaxed than I can remember feeling for ages. And at night, in the hut, which Al very kindly let me stay in while he slept under the stars, I had, by far, the best sleep I've had in years.

You've probably noticed that I haven't mentioned the bathroom facilities. Perhaps that's for the best!

UNIT 5 Money and shopping

5A LANGUAGE

GRAMMAR: Zero and first conditional; future time clauses

1 Complete the sentences with the verbs in the box.

> don't work   work   won't work   works
> will pay   pay   pays   won't pay

1 I'll cut the grass every week if you _____ me.
2 We get seven dollars for each kilo of fruit we pick. If you _____ hard, you can earn a lot.
3 Rafi can have the watch as soon as she _____ me for it.
4 If Alex doesn't offer us enough cash, we _____ for him.
5 Anna won't pass her exams unless she _____ harder.
6 If Marco isn't prepared to do as much as his colleagues, we _____ him.
7 We have no other choice. If we _____ , we don't eat – it's that simple!
8 If they finish the job by the end of the day, I _____ them extra.

2 Use the prompts to complete zero or first conditionals or future time clauses. Include commas where necessary.

1 I _____ me to. (not call you/again today/unless/want)
2 If you _____ you one. (not have/raincoat/I/lend)
3 Ed's so shy. If you _____ bright red. (try/speak to him/usually/go)
4 Your hands _____ gloves. (get cold/if/not wear)
5 You've broken Rick's guitar! He _____! (be/really angry/when/find out)
6 Mom _____ my room. (not let/me/go out/until/clean)

VOCABULARY: Money

3 Match the underlined words with the words in the box.

> mortgage   bill   cash   loan   taxes   coin   broke   wealthy

1 I do some jobs for my neighbor, and he pays me in paper and metal money. _____
2 She must be rich – she has three houses. _____
3 You have to put a piece of metal money into the machine to make it work. _____
4 I want to buy a new car, so I'm going to ask the bank for a sum of money I have to pay back. _____
5 He couldn't go to the restaurant because he was completely without any money. _____
6 Do you think that rich people should pay more money that goes to the government? _____
7 Half of their wages go to paying the money they owe the bank for their house. _____
8 Inside the card was a $50 piece of paper money. _____

4 Complete the second sentence to mean the same as the first.

1 Eva let Kris have $15 until Friday.
   Eva _____ Kris $15 until Friday.
2 Petra got $30 from the ATM.
   Petra _____ out $30 from the ATM.
3 Rochelle bought us each a pizza.
   Rochelle _____ for our pizzas.
4 Peter lent Ollie the train fare.
   Ollie _____ the train fare from Peter.
5 Clara gave Wes the money she owed him.
   Clara _____ Wes back.
6 Janie bought the jacket with her credit card.
   Janie _____ for the jacket by credit card.
7 Yolanda deposited the money into her savings account.
   Yolanda _____ the money into her savings account.

PRONUNCIATION: Intonation

5 ▶5.1 Listen and repeat the sentences. Pay attention to the falling intonation.

1 If John and I go out, it's usually to the theater.
2 We'll be late if you don't hurry.
3 I won't go to the show unless Kate wants to.
4 If it's too warm, I'll open the window.
5 Molly gets angry if we tease her.
6 I'll talk to Dan if I see him.

26

SKILLS 5B

READING: Identifying opinions

Buy Nothing Day

A Did you know that next Saturday is international "Buy Nothing Day"? No, me neither until an e-mail from an anti-consumerist group popped into my inbox yesterday. Apparently, the idea is that we should all keep our cash firmly in our pockets for one day, just to show the big corporations that they don't control us completely.

B I went out to the mall in downtown Santiago, to see what shoppers there think of the idea. First, I met Camila, a 20-year-old student, struggling with armloads of new purchases. "As far as I'm concerned, the whole idea sounds a bit ridiculous," she told me. "If I don't go shopping this Saturday, I'll just buy even more next week instead."

C Javier, who works in a phone store, disagrees. "If you ask me, we all consume far too much, and we could benefit from stopping, even for just one day. Campaigns like this could be a useful way of making people more aware of their own actions. Too many people are making themselves miserable by wasting money on stuff they don't even need."

D Tamara, eighteen, was the only person I spoke to who had actually heard of Buy Nothing Day. "I took part in something called a 'zombie walk' last year," she told me. "The idea was that advertising kills people's brains and turns them into the living dead – like zombies! We all walked around a department store dressed up like dead people, getting in everyone else's way." And does she have similar plans this year? "To be honest, I don't think it was that effective. The same people are organizing a mass credit card cut-up, but I won't be taking part."

E Camila looks at Tamara in amazement. "Cutting up my credit card would be like cutting off a hand for me!" she laughs. "I can't see how anyone lives without one." "I wish more people would cut up their cards," Javier says quietly. "It seems to me that we're so busy worrying about whether we have the smartest clothes or the newest phones, we forget about the important things in life, like friends and family and culture." He stops and laughs, "But please don't tell my boss I said that!"

1 Read the text quickly. Are the statements true or false?

1 Most of the young people in the text like the idea of Buy Nothing Day. _____
2 The "zombie walk" expresses a similar idea to Buy Nothing Day. _____
3 Javier's boss would be pleased to support Buy Nothing Day. _____

2 Read the text again and decide who has the following opinions. Write C for Camila, J for Javier, T for Tamara, or N if nobody expresses the opinion.

1 Buy Nothing Day is a silly idea. _____
2 Companies' profits go down on Buy Nothing Day. _____
3 It would be good for everyone to buy less. _____
4 Events like Buy Nothing Day can make people think about their behavior. _____
5 People often get into debt because they buy too much. _____
6 Shoppers become unhappy when they buy goods that are unnecessary. _____
7 The zombie walk wasn't very effective. _____
8 It is necessary for most people to have a credit card. _____
9 Destroying your credit card is a good idea. _____
10 We place too much importance on buying things. _____

3 Complete each sentence with *even* or *just*. Then match the uses of *even* and *just* with meanings a–f.

1 You need to wait here _____ for one minute. _____
2 George earns a lot, but his brother is _____ more wealthy. _____
3 Katie took my bike, and she didn't _____ ask. _____
4 We all managed to climb the mountain – _____ Rod! _____
5 This jacket is _____ what I need for winter. _____
6 To get a cup of coffee, you _____ press this button. _____

a expressing surprise
b *exactly*
c *simply*
d *only*
e emphasizing a negative
f emphasizing a comparison

5C LANGUAGE

GRAMMAR: Predictions: *will, be going to, may/might*

1 Read the sentences and match statements 1–6 with meanings a–f.

1 It's impossible for Ava to get more points than the leader now. ____
2 Ava's doing better than I expected now. ____
3 There's only one more round, and Ava's well ahead of the other competitors. ____
4 Ava will be competing against more skilled and more experienced people. ____
5 Ava's great, but there's one other competitor who's as good as her. ____
6 I can't think of anyone who's better than Ava. ____

   a She might win the competition.
   b She probably won't win the competition.
   c She might not win the competition.
   d She's not going to win the competition.
   e I'm sure she'll win the competition.
   f She looks like she's going to win the competition.

2 Complete the conversation with *will/won't, going to,* or *might* and verbs from the box. There may be more than one answer.

   write   enjoy   be (x 5)   have   send

   A Everyone's worked so hard on next Friday's concert. It's definitely ¹_____ the best one ever!
   B That's great news!
   A In fact, we've sold so many tickets, I'm worried that we ²_____ enough space.
   B Do you think Rex Brown ³_____ a review for the local paper?
   A I hope so. And we've also had an enthusiastic e-mail from a music magazine, so I think they ⁴_____ a journalist, too.
   B I hope you ⁵_____ too nervous on the night of the concert.
   A I don't think it ⁶_____ too bad because everyone in the audience ⁷_____ a fan.
   B I wish I wasn't working that night. But if I leave early I ⁸_____ able to see the second half.
   A Please try to come. I'm sure you ⁹_____ it!

VOCABULARY: Shopping

3 Complete the sentences with the words and phrases in the box.

   salesclerk   sold out   in-store   checkout
   reasonable   sale   in stock

1 If something is _____, it is available to buy immediately.
2 The job of a _____ is to serve customers in a store.
3 If the price of a product is _____, it is worth at least as much as you paid for it.
4 When products are being sold for less than usual, they are on _____.
5 When there is no more left to buy of a product, it is _____.
6 _____ shopping is done in a store rather than online.
7 The place where you pay for your shopping is the _____.

4 Complete the conversation with shopping words.

   Zack   Going shopping is so tiring! It's much easier to sit in an armchair and ¹b_____ loads of different websites.
   Harvey But I much prefer to see things before I buy them.
   Zack   That's why I usually ²o_____ a few things and choose the best one.
   Harvey But then you have to ³r_____ the ones you don't want – I just can't be bothered! And I think online shopping encourages people to buy too much. It's too easy to put lots of ⁴i_____ in your ⁵b_____. In a store, you know you're going to have to carry them home, and it feels more real.
   Zack   But I think online shopping actually saves you money. You can check the price of a ⁶p_____ on different sites to make sure you get the best deal.
   Harvey The other important thing for me is that once I've bought something, I can have it immediately – I don't like waiting!
   Zack   Yeah, but lots of sites have free next-day ⁷d_____, and you don't have to carry anything home!

PRONUNCIATION: Word stress

5 ▶5.2 Read the sentences aloud. Remember to pronounce *probably* with two syllables and *definitely* with three syllables. Listen and repeat.

1 She probably won't answer.
2 The weather will probably get better.
3 You'll definitely pass your exams.
4 Becky is probably going to come later.
5 Dad definitely won't be happy.
6 It's definitely not going to snow.

SKILLS 5D

SPEAKING: Explaining what's wrong

1 ▶ 5.3 Gisela works in a clothing store. Listen to her conversations with two customers and complete the sentences.

1 The woman's T-shirt doesn't _____. It's too _____.
2 Gisela offers her a smaller _____.
3 The woman asks for a _____.
4 She doesn't have the _____.
5 She agrees to _____ it for a smaller T-shirt.
6 The second customer would like to _____ a coat.
7 The coat is _____ on the inside.
8 He has changed his mind about the coat and doesn't _____ it any more.

2 Match items a–e with problems 1–5.

1 It's scratched. _____
2 It keeps crashing. _____
3 There's something wrong with the back wheel. _____
4 It's too tight. _____
5 There are some pieces missing. _____

   a jigsaw
   b tablet
   c CD
   d shirt
   e bicycle

3 Complete the conversation with the words in the box. There are three extra words.

> work   possible   missing   broken   could
> exchange   wrong   return   like   model

A Can I help you, sir?
B ¹_____ I ²_____ this camera, please?
A Is there a problem with it, sir?
B Yes. It doesn't ³_____.
A Not at all?
B No. I can't even get it to turn on. I think there's something ⁴_____ with the "on" button.
A May I look? Oh yes, I think it's ⁵_____. I'll get you another one.
B I think I'd ⁶_____ a refund, if that's ⁷_____.
A Certainly, sir.

4 For 1–6, use your own ideas to explain what is wrong or to say what you would like to happen. Do not use the same phrase twice.

1 I'm returning these headphones.
_____
Could I exchange them for another pair, please?
2 I'd like to return this jacket. It's too big.
_____
3 Could I return this video game?
_____
I'd like another one, if that's possible.
4 I'd like to return this flashlight. It's broken.
_____
5 I bought this printer last week, and it doesn't work.
_____
6 I'd like to exchange these pants, please.
_____

5 REVIEW and PRACTICE

HOME   BLOG   **PODCASTS**   ABOUT   CONTACT

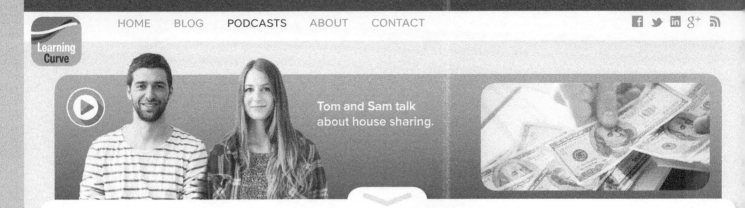

Tom and Sam talk about house sharing.

LISTENING

1 🔊 5.4 Listen to the podcast and check (✓) the correct sentences.

a James said he didn't have any money. _____
b Jessica and her roommate always refused to lend James any money. _____
c Jessica and her roommate often gave James money. _____
d Jessica and her roommate told James's parents about the problem. _____
e In the end, James gave Jessica and her roommate the money he owed them. _____

2 🔊 5.4 Listen again and complete the sentences with one or two words.

1 Sam gives an example of a mean roommate who argues about the gas or _____.
2 Tom complains that Sam never buys the _____.
3 Jessica shared a house with two other people when she was in _____.
4 Jessica and her roommate often _____ James money, but he didn't pay them back.
5 Jessica used to feel guilty when she saw that James had nothing _____.
6 James's parents were _____.
7 Jessica told James that she would _____ his parents.
8 Jessica thinks that James asked someone for a _____ so that he could pay back the money he owed.

READING

1 Read Kate's blog on page 31 and choose the best summary.

Kate wants to

a stop wasting her money on products that she does not need.
b spend less so that she can save enough money for a vacation.
c buy nothing during the month of January.

2 Choose the correct options to complete the sentences.

1 Kate thinks that the people who read her blog
  a won't believe she can change her spending habits.
  b will think that it will be easy for her to change her spending habits.
  c will try to help her change her spending habits.
2 Kate's goal is to
  a get Simon's permission before she buys anything.
  b have enough money for an exciting vacation abroad.
  c only buy things that cost less than $30.
3 Simon will help Kate by
  a always going shopping with her.
  b giving her advice about what she should and should not buy.
  c stopping her from buying anything.
4 According to Kate, 30 percent of people who shop using their cell phone
  a buy sports gear.
  b do this while they are at the doctor's.
  c do this while they are waiting.
5 It is clear that Simon has told Kate
  a to send some unnecessary items back to the company.
  b never to buy yoga pants.
  c not to use her cell phone to shop.
6 When Kate tries on clothes, she
  a never thinks she looks nice in the mirror.
  b thinks she always looks fantastic.
  c always takes advice from the staff in the store.

HOME BLOG PODCASTS ABOUT CONTACT

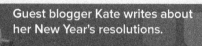

Guest blogger Kate writes about her New Year's resolutions.

My January goals

OK, I'm a week or so late with these, but better late than never! As it's the time of year for New Year's resolutions, I've decided to make a fresh start with my finances. Yes, friends, it may be a huge challenge for someone like me, but I'm going to try to change the spending habits of a lifetime! (Now, don't look at me like that – I'll become a saver, not a spender – you'll see!) And **here's how:** I now have a "money buddy." His name is Simon, and this is how it works. I've told Simon about my aim for this year – to save up enough money to go skydiving in the summer in Lake Wanaka, New Zealand. Simon and I have agreed that if I want to buy a big item, I'll ask him first. Simply, I won't buy anything costing over $30 unless he says I can. Those of you who have met Simon know that he's pretty strict, so he should be good in this role! (He's already made me return some shoes that I bought in December.☹)

No more browsing while waiting! Now, I'm clearly not alone in this habit. Apparently, 30 percent of people who use their cell phones to shop do so while waiting in line. This is a habit that I'm *totally* going to break. *This month*! No more browsing sports gear while I'm in the doctor's waiting room because we all know what happens when I do that … (And, yes, Simon, I'm returning those two pairs of yoga pants that I don't need. They're in the mail right now, on their way back to the company.)

No visiting the shopping malls. At least when I order something online, there's no salesclerk to tell me that I look fantastic in whatever piece of clothing I'm trying on! (And I'm the kind of person who believes what the salesclerks say, even when the mirror tells a different story!)

No taking advantage of discounts, even when they seem amazing. And for anyone else who struggles when items are on sale, let me pass on my money buddy's words of wisdom: "If you don't *need* something, you're wasting your money when you buy, it *whatever* the price."

If I do all these things, I'll definitely be able to save enough money for my trip to New Zealand. So wish me luck, readers, and I'll check in next month to let you know how I'm doing.

UNIT 6 Work and education

6A LANGUAGE

GRAMMAR: Present perfect and simple past, *already, yet, recently*

1 Complete the sentences with the verbs in the box.

> have you done   have lived   went
> hasn't been   did you do
> didn't go   lived   has been

1 Vicky _____ to Buenos Aires twice this year.
2 _____ your homework yet?
3 I wonder why Laura _____ to see us recently?
4 Carol and Dom's house is in Barcelona. They _____ in Spain for several years now.
5 When he was a child, Rory _____ with his grandparents.
6 Jake _____ to Tokyo for two weeks last spring.
7 _____ any surfing while you were in Australia?
8 Rose _____ to Owen's party last weekend.

2 Complete the text with the present perfect or simple past form of the verbs in parentheses.

> My father ¹_____ (work) in Kenya for five years when I was a child, and we all went with him. My parents ²_____ (be) back every two years since then, but since I ³_____ (start) work three years ago, I ⁴_____ (not be) able to go with them. Unfortunately, I'm not free when they're going this year either, so I ⁵_____ (decide) to go on my own.
> I still have a couple of good friends in Nairobi, and although I ⁶_____ (not see) them for a few years, we keep in touch by e-mail and Skype. I ⁷_____ (get) a wonderful letter from one of them last week, offering to take me to Nairobi National Park. I'm really excited because I ⁸_____ (never be) there before.

VOCABULARY: Work and careers (1)

3 Match sentences 1–7 with a–g.

1 They gave Ravi a better job with more money. _____
2 Hamza spent a week away from the office learning how to design a website. _____
3 When Aidan was 65, he stopped working. _____
4 Jack worked for an electronics company as part of his degree. _____
5 Rick's job wasn't needed any more, and he had to leave the company. _____
6 Ivan worked at a local newspaper before he applied for a job with a national paper. _____
7 Alex decided to leave his job. _____

a He took a training course.
b He did a job placement.
c He resigned.
d He retired.
e He got experience first.
f He got a promotion.
g He was laid off.

4 Complete the words for work and careers.

1 Now I've got so much experience, I deserve to get a p_____.
2 Ayesha got f_____ for doing online shopping at work.
3 I'm going to college to get the s_____ I need to become a translator.
4 Do you believe that politicians who lie should r_____?
5 Paloma managed to get an i_____ with a fashion magazine during her summer vacation.
6 I need to earn some cash. Where's the best place to l_____ for a job?

PRONUNCIATION: Present perfect and simple past

5 ▶ 6.1 Listen and complete the sentences with verbs in the present perfect or simple past. Then listen again and repeat.

1 I _____ Ethan to come to the meeting.
2 David _____ to Mexico last year.
3 They _____ a horse.
4 I _____ my friend to help me.
5 Did you know that Scott _____ to Chicago?
6 They _____ a new car.

SKILLS 6B

LISTENING: Understanding specific information

1 Before you listen to the conversation about Megan's future education, match questions 1–10 with the information you need (a–j).

1 What is Sue Kerridge's job? _____
2 What is Megan's dad's name? _____
3 How does Megan feel about school? _____
4 Why does her dad want her to go to college? _____
5 How much more can people with college degrees earn? _____
6 What does Megan enjoy doing when she needs to? _____
7 What does Sue suggest Megan should do before she decides about her future? _____
8 What sort of engineering company does she mention, in particular? _____
9 Do people doing internships usually earn more than people with a normal job? _____
10 What does Megan think of Sue's suggestion? _____

a an amount of money
b a word that shows an emotion
c a piece of advice
d a reason for something
e the name of a job
f an opinion
g a comparison
h an activity
i a person's name
j a type of company

2 ▶ 6.2 Listen to the conversation. Complete these answers to exercise 1.

1 She's a _____ _____.
2 _____ Briscoe.
3 She _____ it.
4 In order to have a rewarding _____.
5 An extra _____.
6 She fixes her own _____.
7 She suggests an _____ with an _____ company.
8 An _____ engineering company.
9 No, they don't usually earn as _____ as other employees.
10 She thinks it sounds _____.

3 ▶ 6.3 <u>Underline</u> the words you think will be stressed. Listen and check.

1 Going to one of the top colleges will help you get a well-paid job.
2 College isn't necessarily the best choice for everyone.
3 It's a good idea to get some work experience before you decide on a career.
4 Will wants to work as a science teacher.
5 You will need to get some more skills.
6 Some supermarkets offer training courses for future managers.

4 Complete the sentences.

1 An _____ is someone who works for someone else.
2 We usually send a _____ letter with a CV.
3 If you are _____ for something at work, you have to make sure it happens or is done.
4 Your working _____ are the circumstances that affect your job.
5 _____ jobs do not last for a fixed period of time.
6 A _____ job is one that you get satisfaction from.
7 A person who is _____ does not have a job.
8 In a _____ job, you have to do a lot of different things.

6C LANGUAGE

GRAMMAR: Present perfect continuous and present perfect

1 Choose the correct options to complete the sentences.

1. Ed has ____ his friend's birthday every year for the last 40 years.
   a remembered   b been remembering
2. How long have you ____ studying today?
   a been   b been spending
3. Gaby has ____ the house all morning.
   a cleaned   b been cleaning
4. I hope you haven't ____ very long.
   a waiting   b been waiting
5. Rex has ____ a member of this club for almost five years.
   a been   b been being
6. My parents have ____ this house since 1998.
   a owned   b been owning
7. I'm so tired – I've ____ wood for the fire.
   a chopped   b been chopping
8. What has Marta ____? She's covered in mud!
   a done   b been doing

2 Complete the conversation with the verbs in the box. Use the present perfect continuous or present perfect form.

| practice | know | mean | have |
| take | not learn | play | |

Federika Hey, Adam! Is that your guitar? I didn't know you played.
Adam Well I ¹____ for very long, and I'm not very good yet. You have a guitar, too, don't you?
Federika Yes, I do. I ²____ it since I was four. In fact, my band has a concert next week – do you want to come?
Adam Sure, I'd love to. Are you nervous about playing?
Federika A bit. I ³____ for weeks, but some of the songs are really difficult, and I'm still getting used to my new guitar. I ⁴____ it for a couple of months now, but it still feels strange. By the way, do you have a teacher?
Adam Well, I ⁵____ classes with a man my sister recommended, but I don't like him that much. Do you know anyone good?
Federika You should try Fergus Jones. I ⁶____ him for years, and he's great. In fact, I'll call him for you if you'd like – I ⁷____ to get in touch with him for ages.

VOCABULARY: Education

3 Read the sentences and check (✓) True or False.

1	Students usually have to pay to go to a public school.	True	False
2	A term is a period of time when students are in school.	True	False
3	You become a graduate when you start studying at a college.	True	False
4	Principals teach the oldest children in a school.	True	False
5	If you cheat on an exam, you do something that is not allowed.	True	False
6	"Taking notes" means getting written information from your teacher.	True	False
7	If you hand in work, you give it to your teacher.	True	False
8	Students are likely to get into trouble if they don't do their homework.	True	False
9	A schedule is a list of school dates, but not times.	True	False
10	Children usually start elementary school when they are 16.	True	False

4 Complete the sentences with education words.

1. The students behave in Mr. Gallagher's class. They have to, because he is very s_____.
2. My girlfriend teaches politics in college. She's a l_____.
3. Lola isn't at home during the semester because she goes to b_____ s_____.
4. Gustavo's at the University of São Paulo doing a d_____ in Engineering.
5. Samira's studying in the library because she has to r_____ her notes for an important exam.
6. Anna's daughter is three, so she just started n_____ s_____.
7. Ian's parents saved all their money in order to send him to a p_____ s_____.
8. Ben worked really hard on his essay, and his teacher gave him a g_____ g_____.
9. Astrid had to take her exams again because she f_____ them the first time.
10. We get our g_____ next week – I'm so nervous because I need to pass this course!

PRONUNCIATION: Weak form of *been*

5 ▶ 6.4 Listen and repeat. Pay attention to the pronunciation of *been* and the way the words are stressed.

1. She hasn't been married for long.
2. I've been hoping to meet her.
3. The children have been playing.
4. Have you been talking to Luca?
5. Veronica's been complaining again.
6. Kyle's been having problems at work.

SKILLS 6D

WRITING: Writing a cover letter

SUMMER CAMP COUNSELORS NEEDED FOR LANGUAGE SCHOOL

Sunshine School provides summer camps for over 1,000 teenagers from around the world. We aim to develop their language skills in a comfortable, safe, but fun environment.

Counselors' duties include:
- organizing sports and art activities
- accompanying students on cultural visits
- supervising meal times

Candidates should:
- be reliable and friendly
- work well as part of a team
- be energetic and enthusiastic
- have excellent written and spoken English

A knowledge of one or more foreign languages and good IT skills would be an advantage.

To apply, please send your CV to David Green, explaining why you are interested in this position. Please provide details of your qualifications, skills, and any relevant experience.

1 Read Lulu's cover letter. Complete 1–11 with the correct prepositions.

Dear Mr. Green,

I am writing to apply ¹_____ the position of Summer Camp Counselor. My CV's attached to this e-mail. I am currently doing a degree ²_____ psychology. I am particularly interested ³_____ working with young people in the future, so I believe that working ⁴_____ a summer camp counselor would be the ideal job for me.
I am passionate ⁵_____ travel and language learning because they help people from different countries understand each other. I am proficient ⁶_____ Spanish and Russian, and I'm trying to learn Japanese at the moment. I believe that my knowledge of languages would help me communicate well with your students.
Last year, I had a summer job with the city youth program. I enjoyed working as part of a group that was responsible ⁷_____ sports activities. I worked with children from different backgrounds and helped to support children who found group activities difficult. It was wonderful! In addition, I babysat once a week, which shows that I am a reliable person. I have loads of energy, and I love working with other people. I believe that this, together with my experience, makes me ideal ⁸_____ the role, and I would very much welcome the opportunity to work ⁹_____ your organization.
Thank you ¹⁰_____ considering my application.
I look forward ¹¹_____ hearing from you.

All the best,
Lulu Ramirez

2 Check (✓) the points from the job ad that Lulu includes in her letter.

1 organizing sports activities _____
2 organizing art activities _____
3 accompanying students on cultural visits _____
4 supervising meal times _____
5 being reliable _____
6 being friendly _____
7 working well as part of a team _____
8 being energetic _____
9 being enthusiastic _____
10 having excellent written and spoken English _____
11 knowing other languages _____
12 having good IT skills _____

3 Rewrite the underlined sentences from Lulu's cover letter in a more formal style.

1 My CV's attached to this e-mail.
_____

2 I'm trying to learn Japanese at the moment.
_____

3 It was wonderful!
_____

4 I've got loads of energy, and I love working with other people.
_____

5 All the best,
_____

4 The same school is looking for someone to arrange transportation from the airport for adult students arriving in the U.S. during July and August.

Read the job description below and write a cover letter to David Green, applying for that job. Remember to provide details of your qualifications, skills, and any relevant experience.

Duties include:
- reserving buses and cabs to meet students at U.S. airports
- contacting host families to arrange accommodations for students

Candidates should:
- have a good level of education
- have a polite, confident telephone manner
- be extremely well-organized and reliable
- be prepared to work on weekends

6 REVIEW and PRACTICE

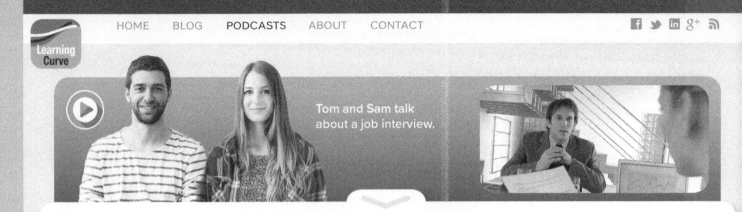

LISTENING

1 ▶ 6.5 Listen to the podcast and check (✓) the words that you hear.

a varied ____
b stressful ____
c skills ____
d well-paid ____
e rewarding ____
f career ____
g application form ____
h part-time ____
i full-time ____
j permanent ____

2 ▶ 6.5 Listen again and choose the correct options to complete the sentences.

1 After an interview, Tom once accidentally
 a started a fire.
 b made an alarm start.
 c broke a window.

2 Patrick has been trying to find a new job for
 a eighteen months.
 b twelve months.
 c six months.

3 Patrick has had his present job for about
 a half a year.
 b three years.
 c three and a half years.

4 Patrick's friend
 a used to work for the computer company.
 b started working for the company five years ago.
 c has applied for the same job as Patrick.

5 During the interview, Patrick noticed that
 a the man was reading his application form.
 b the woman was reading his application form.
 c both interviewers were reading his application form.

6 Patrick explained that he wasn't applying for
 a a full-time job.
 b a permanent job.
 c the position of telephone sales representative.

READING

1 Read Jack's blog on page 37 and choose the best summary.

a College is not the best way to get a good job.
b You need work experience to get a good job.
c College is not the only way to get a good job.

2 Check (✓) the correct sentences.

1 Jack is very happy for the young people who are going to go to college. ____
2 Jack says that you do not need a college degree to get a good job. ____
3 Will studied at a public school. ____
4 Will always listened carefully during his classes. ____
5 Will didn't get any experience cooking on his first job in a restaurant. ____
6 All of the restaurants that Will worked in were successful. ____
7 In one of his jobs, Will had to do the same task all the time. ____
8 One of Will's bosses realized that he was talented and gave him a more important job. ____

3 Use words and phrases from the blog to complete sentences 1–6.

1 My father was very depressed after he was _____ _____.
2 If I _____ _____ _____, I will earn more money.
3 My son got excellent _____, so we went to a restaurant to celebrate.
4 I took a _____ _____ to learn new skills.
5 I wanted to _____ _____ of work before I finished college, so I always got a job during the summer.
6 I got my _____ in history, so I became a history teacher.

36

REVIEW and PRACTICE 6

HOME BLOG PODCASTS ABOUT CONTACT

Guest blogger Jack talks about alternatives to college.

Where there's a Will ...

During the next few weeks, young people across the country will graduate from high school. Some will spend the next four years getting a degree in college. Congratulations to those bright young people! I know how hard they've all been working for the last several years. I hope they've gotten the grades they need to continue with their education and sincerely wish them all the best with their studies.

However, I think it's worth reminding any young readers out there that a college education isn't the *only* route to a successful career.

Take my business partner, Will, for example. Will was sixteen when he left school. (This was allowed in his state!) His parents had sent him to an expensive private school where the poor guy kept getting into trouble for not paying attention in class. He wasn't a *bad boy*, you understand – I mean he never misbehaved really badly or did anything terrible. He just wasn't very interested in the subjects that he was being taught. (Probably rather disappointing for his poor parents who, I'm sure, only wanted the best for him!)

However, there was one topic that Will was *extremely* interested in learning about when he was a teenager – one thing that he was prepared to work *really hard* at. And that topic was FOOD. For as long as he can remember, he's loved cooking (and of course eating!). When the other boys were kicking a ball around in the park, Will was in the kitchen, looking through his mom's recipe books (or, when she allowed it, cooking!). As soon as he was old enough, he got a weekend job, washing dishes in a restaurant, just so that he could experience a professional kitchen. While his classmates were studying for exams, Will was busy loading plates into huge, industrial dishwashers. He's worked in a kitchen ever since.

Will's career path has twisted and turned – that's to be expected. The work has been exhausting – and, no doubt, stressful. In the early years, he was laid off several times because the restaurants he was working in weren't making enough money. At one stage, he was holding two part-time jobs, just to earn enough money. In another job, he spent ten hours a day, six days a week, preparing vegetables. But after a year in that job, his manager recognized his ability (or at least his enthusiasm!), and he got a promotion. And all this time, he was learning new skills and getting valuable experience.

Will didn't get a formal degree – in fact, he's never even taken a training course – but last year, he and I finally bought our own restaurant together. Congratulations, Will – I'm so proud of you!

UNIT 7

Entertainment

7A LANGUAGE

GRAMMAR: The passive

1 Choose the correct options to complete the sentences.

1 I don't have a computer at the moment. It _____.
   a is fixing   b is being fixed
   c fixes

2 Last year, he _____ in a traffic accident.
   a was injured   b injured
   c was being injured

3 Unwanted items can _____ to us at the above address.
   a be returning   b be returned
   c return

4 Sadly, much of the forest has now _____.
   a destroy   b destroyed
   c been destroyed

5 They just announced that the flight _____ by two hours.
   a is delaying   b will be delayed
   c will delay

6 The kitchen _____ at the moment.
   a is painted   b painting
   c is being painted

7 So much progress _____ in so little time.
   a been achieved   b has achieved
   c has been achieved

8 How much of your food _____ each week?
   a throws away   b is throwing away
   c is thrown away

2 Complete the sentences using the verbs in the box in the passive form with the prompts in parentheses.

| film   ring   invent   punish |
| announce   advise   decorate |

1 We can't go in the living room because it _____. (present continuous)

2 The electric battery _____ by Alessandro Volta. (simple past)

3 Those bells _____ at eleven o'clock every morning. (simple present)

4 She _____ by her doctor to stop taking the pills. (present perfect)

5 The results of the competition _____ as I arrived. (past continuous)

6 Some early scenes in the movie _____ in the studio. (future with *will*)

7 People _____ for their crimes. (+ *must*)

VOCABULARY: Movies

3 Order the letters to make movie words.

Zara So what movie did you see last night?
Raf   It was a Spanish movie, ¹ **tse** _____ in Madrid. It's a ² **leesqu** _____ to a movie that I saw last year.
Zara I didn't know you spoke Spanish!
Raf   I don't. But it had ³ **ibustlest** _____.
Zara I prefer it when foreign films are ⁴ **budbed** _____. Anyway, was it good?
Raf   The ⁵ **satc** _____ was fantastic, especially the main actor. It had a pretty complicated ⁶ **tolp** _____ that was sometimes hard to follow. What have you seen recently?
Zara I saw a ⁷ **rorohr** _____ movie last week.
Raf   Oh no, I can't stand blood!
Zara I know, but it was good, and really funny at times.
Raf   Who wrote the ⁸ **tcrisp** _____ for it?
Zara I don't know, but the main character was ⁹ **depaly** _____ by Douglas Booth. And the ¹⁰ **nostudrack** _____ was amazing. I've been listening to it on my headphones all morning.

4 Complete the movie words.

1 Ian likes ac_____ _____ _____ movies with lots of fights.

2 The movie will be re_____ _____ _____ _____ _____ next spring.

3 The movie's special ef_____ _____ _____ _____ were amazing, especially the ones in space.

4 We watched a do_____ _____ _____ _____ about the final years of the artist's life.

5 The wedding sc_____ _____ _____ at the end was hilarious.

6 My favorite movies are ba_____ _____ _____ on real-life stories.

7 It was a science-fi_____ _____ _____ _____ movie, set in the 25th century.

8 Sarah knows all the songs from that mu_____ _____ _____ _____.

PRONUNCIATION: Past participles

5 ▶ 7.1 Match the vowels in the underlined words with a–d. Say the sentences aloud. Then listen, check, and repeat.

a /oʊ/   b /ɑ/   c /ʌ/   d /ɔ/

1 Both movies had been <u>dubbed</u> into Italian. ____
2 The movie was <u>watched</u> by 9.2 million viewers. ____
3 Which actor was <u>chosen</u> to play the part? ____
4 Her lines were <u>spoken</u> by a different person. ____
5 The movie <u>won</u> three Oscars. ____
6 The plot is about a <u>lost</u> astronaut. ____

SKILLS 7B

READING: Guessing the meaning of words from context

The best method?

While Daniel Day-Lewis was playing the lead role in the movie *Lincoln*, he is reported to have started signing his text messages "A" for Abraham, so entangled had his identity become with his screen character. His friends found ᵃthis strange, but it was all part of the way he worked.

Day-Lewis was practicing "method acting," a technique developed by the Russian actor and director Konstantin Stanislavski. Ideas about method acting have evolved over the years, but the central aim has always been for the actor to achieve complete emotional identification with the character he or she is playing. In practice, ᵇthat often means preparing for a role by having the same experiences as the character or, at the very least, making an effort to learn as much as possible about such experiences.

Such preparations can take many forms. Actors may move to another country and immerse themselves in an unfamiliar culture. They might learn a language or a skill such as horseriding or playing a musical instrument, or interview people who witnessed a particular event. Some actors, however, take things further. Much, much further. Christian Bale, for example, shed a massive 28 kilos to play Trevor Reznik, a man with severe psychological problems, in *The Machinist*, while Jamie Foxx actually glued his eyes together to bring added authenticity to his role as the blind musician Ray Charles. However, it was so uncomfortable that he soon gave ᶜthis up.

Probably the most famous recent example of extreme method acting is Leonardo DiCaprio in *The Revenant*. DiCaprio put himself through an unbelievably punishing regime of sleeping out in the wilderness, swimming in freezing rivers, and even eating the raw flesh of a bison (and he's a vegetarian!). ᵈThat gave him a real taste of the life he was about to portray.

Sadly for him, however, not everyone appreciated his efforts, with some people seeing them primarily as an attempt to gain the Oscar that had been eluding him for so long. ᵉThis meant that the Internet was soon awash with spoof posters showing DiCaprio's character in various desperate situations, with captions such as: "Do this man a favor. Just give him his Oscar!"

---

1 Read the article and choose the best options to complete the sentences.

1. Daniel Day-Lewis wrote "A" on his texts because
   a. he admired Abraham Lincoln so much.
   b. he confused himself with Abraham Lincoln.
   c. he didn't want people to know who they were from.

2. In method acting, the actor aims to
   a. look as much like the character as possible.
   b. use a range of different acting methods.
   c. think the same way as the character.

3. If a movie is about a particular event in history, the actor can find out more by
   a. reading interviews with people who were there.
   b. learning more about history.
   c. talking to people who were there.

4. Leonardo DiCaprio suffered a lot because
   a. his director wanted the scenes to look realistic.
   b. he wanted to have a better understanding of his character.
   c. he thought it would make people see the movie.

5. Some people joked about DiCaprio's method acting because
   a. they thought that his acting still wasn't good enough to win an Oscar.
   b. they didn't believe that what he did was very difficult.
   c. they thought he was making it obvious that he wanted an Oscar.

2 Find the words in bold in the text. Look at the immediate context and choose the best options.

1. If two things are **entangled**, they are *joined together / damaging one another / difficult to understand*.
2. If something **evolves**, it *changes completely / changes suddenly / changes gradually*.
3. If you **immerse** yourself in something, you *spend a lot of time doing or experiencing it / try to copy it / strongly dislike it*.
4. **Authenticity** means being *impressive / real / painful*.
5. If something **eludes** you, you *want it very much / almost achieve it / do not manage to achieve it*.
6. A **spoof** is a *humorous version / a criticism / an illegal version* of something.

3 Match a–e (*this* and *that*) in the text with meanings 1–8. There are three extra meanings.

1. the fact that method acting has changed ____
2. writing "A" on his text messages ____
3. learning to ride a horse or play an instrument ____
4. sticking his eyes together ____
5. trying to understand a character's emotions very thoroughly ____
6. people thinking he wanted an Oscar ____
7. the fact that he has never won an Oscar ____
8. doing physically difficult things ____

7C LANGUAGE

GRAMMAR: Modals of ability and possibility

1 Order the words to make sentences.

1 to / paint / to / she'd / able / like / be
   _____.

2 able / never / to / swim / he's / been
   _____.

3 be / later / call / I'll / you / to / able
   _____.

4 meet / are / to / tonight / able / us / you
   _____?

5 they / see / movie / able / the / weren't / to
   _____.

6 being / ride / he / to / motorcycle / able / a / loves
   _____.

7 we / the / museum / to / be / visit / won't / able
   _____.

8 to / a / haven't / able / I / buy / ticket / been
   _____.

2 Read the sentences and complete the replies with the correct form of *can* or *be able to*. There may be more than one answer.

1 **A** Are you coming to the concert next Saturday?
   B No, I'm afraid we're both working, so we _____.

2 **A** The best thing about vacations is all the books you can read!
   B Yes, I love _____ read all day. It's so relaxing.

3 **A** Why is she taking a math course?
   B She wants _____ help her son when he's older.

4 **A** I didn't know you were injured, Jamie.
   B It's pretty bad. I _____ play any sports since January.

5 **A** Did you ask Ethan about the trip?
   B No, he was in a meeting all day yesterday, so I _____ contact him.

6 **A** I'll bring the groceries back on my bike.
   B Will you _____ manage OK?

7 **A** I heard that Suzi is sick.
   B Yes, she _____ get out of bed for three days.

8 **A** I get so upset when I can't sleep.
   B Me, too! I really hate _____ sleep.

VOCABULARY: TV and music

3 Replace the underlined words with the nouns in the box.

| album | band | track | playlist |
| channel | episode | host | audience |

1 The <u>person who introduces the show</u> got into trouble after being rude to his guest. _____

2 I switched to another <u>TV station</u> to watch a music show. _____

3 I've just downloaded their latest <u>collection of songs</u>. _____

4 Someone from the <u>people watching the show</u> asked him a question. _____

5 I've been watching a series about a boy band; tonight it's the last <u>part of the story</u>. _____

6 What's on your <u>choice of music</u> for the party? _____

7 Which is your favorite <u>group of musicians</u>? _____

8 The second <u>song on the CD</u> is probably the best. _____

4 Complete the sentences with TV and music words.

1 I watched the first episode in the _____, but there are four more parts to go.

2 They had a few successful records, but *Get by* was probably their biggest _____.

3 The next time my favorite singer goes _____ _____, I'm definitely buying a ticket!

4 I have all her music, but I've never seen her perform _____ on stage.

5 He entered a TV _____ _____ and won first prize for singing.

6 There's a new _____ _____ on Channel 4 tonight about people marrying total strangers!

7 My mom loves this _____ _____ about a typical small town. It's been on TV for over twenty years.

8 I can't stand all the _____ they show between TV episode.

PRONUNCIATION: /eɪ/ and /ʊ/ sounds

5 ▶ 7.2 Practice saying the sentences. Make sure that you pronounce the vowel sound in *able* /eɪ/ and the vowel sound in *could* /ʊ/. Listen, check, and repeat.

1 I'd love to be able to play the guitar.
2 The music was so loud I couldn't hear Diego.
3 I won't be able to join you this year.
4 Luckily, I was able to take some time off.
5 She could play three instruments by the time she was ten.
6 We couldn't contact her yesterday.

SKILLS 7D

SPEAKING: Giving directions

1 ▶ 7.3 Frida wants to go to a shoe store. Listen to the two conversations and complete the directions.

First store
1 It's _____ Grover Street.
2 From here, keep _____ _____ until you get to the _____.
3 When you get to the museum, _____ _____.
4 Go _____ the hill and _____ the movie theater on your _____.
5 Royal's is just a little bit farther, on the _____ _____ of the street.

Second store
6 _____ this street to the end.
7 Take a _____ _____ Cooper Street.
8 After that, you need to _____ the _____ _____.
9 It's _____ _____ a pizzeria.

2 Number these sentences 1–8 to make a conversation.

a Yes, it's across from the bus station. ____
b Yes, I did. It's next to a shopping center. ____
c That's right – you've got it! ____
d Of course. Take the first right at the traffic light, then go straight ahead. It's on the right. ____
e Excuse me, do you know where the library is? ____
f Sorry, did you say across from the bus station? ____
g And can you tell me how to get there, please? ____
h So, it's the first right, then straight ahead, and it's on the right? ____

3 Order the words to make indirect questions.

1 tell / you / bank / me / could / is / where / the
_____?
2 bus station / where / you / do / the / is / know
_____?
3 if / know / is / drugstore / near / you / there / a / here / do
_____?
4 name / you / is / the / this / could / tell / what / me / street / of
_____?
5 which / you / museum / could / is / on / tell / street / me / the
_____?
6 bus / this / stadium / know / do / the / stops / you / if / near
_____?

4 ▶ 7.4 Complete the conversation. Then listen and check.

A Sorry to [1]_____ you, but [2]_____ you tell me where the hospital is?
B Yes, it's about ten minutes [3]_____ car from here. You need to drive up Castle Hill, and [4]_____ right when you get to the traffic light.
A So, it's [5]_____ the hill and then make a [6]_____?
B That's right. Then [7]_____ the first left after the big traffic circle. Go [8]_____ ahead [9]_____ you see the hospital [10]_____ the left.
A And do you [11]_____ if I can park there?
B Yes, just [12]_____ the road around and you'll find the parking lot next to the main hospital building.

5 Think of two places in a town or city you know. Write an explanation of how to get from one to the other.

7 REVIEW and PRACTICE

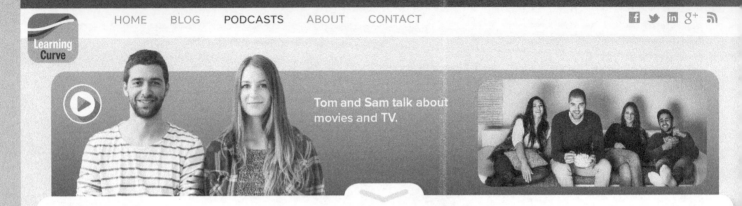

HOME   BLOG   **PODCASTS**   ABOUT   CONTACT

Tom and Sam talk about movies and TV.

LISTENING

1 ▶ 7.5 Listen to the podcast. Check (✓) the statement which is NOT true.

1. Sam prefers watching television to going to the movies. _____
2. Rosie likes television series more than movies. _____
3. Tom has more or less the same opinion as the caller, Rosie. _____

2 ▶ 7.5 Listen again. Are the sentences true (T), false (F) or doesn't say (DS)?

1. In Sam's opinion, it is better to see a movie at the theater. _____
2. Tom and Sam often go to the movies together. _____
3. Rosie thinks that Hollywood likes making original movies. _____
4. In Rosie's opinion, movie companies do not use new writers very often. _____
5. Rosie's favorite directors never make TV series. _____
6. In TV series, there is not enough time to develop the characters. _____
7. Rosie thinks that the best actors always want to act in Hollywood movies. _____

READING

1 Read Kate's blog on page 47 and choose the best summary of what a movie extra does, according to Kate.

a. They never speak and spend most of their time waiting.
b. They almost never speak and spend most of their time waiting.
c. They never speak, and they sometimes do not even appear in the movie.

2 Choose the correct options to complete the sentences.

1. According to Kate, extras
   a. are never recognized by their friends.
   b. usually take part in long science-fiction movies.
   c. usually appear only for a few seconds, often in groups.
2. Kate's mother did not see her daughter in the movie because
   a. she fell asleep at one point.
   b. Kate did not appear in it.
   c. she was too busy to go to the movies.
3. For most of the time, extras
   a. read books.
   b. listen to the director.
   c. do very little.
4. Most scenes in Kate's latest movie take place in
   a. London.
   b. a town outside of New York.
   c. elsewhere in the UK.
5. Kate didn't see any famous actors because
   a. it was too cold.
   b. they weren't in her part of the movie.
   c. they were all in the UK.
6. At the end of her blog, Kate sounds
   a. amused.
   b. disappointed.
   c. embarrassed.

REVIEW and PRACTICE 7

HOME BLOG PODCASTS ABOUT CONTACT

Guest blogger Kate writes about working as a movie extra.

EXTRA SPECIAL

Here's something you may not know about me. Every now and then, I work as an extra on movie sets. Yes, I'm one of those people that you might just see in a crowd when you're watching a movie. Or not … If you don't pay close attention, you'll miss me! In fact, even if you are able to keep your eyes open for the entire movie, you still might not see me. Two years ago, my poor mother sat through one of those incredibly long science-fiction movies, which, as we all know, is her least favorite type of movie, because she wanted to see her daughter being killed by a robot. Sadly, unknown to her (and me), by the time the movie was released, that particular scene had been cut, and my mother had wasted three hours of her busy life.

People often ask me what it's like to work as an extra on a movie set. Well, extras are sometimes referred to as "moving furniture," and this seems about right to me. We don't speak (or rather we rarely speak, although, of course, if we do, we're paid more). We're simply there to provide the background for the main action. Most of our time is spent hanging around, just waiting for the director to tell us when we're needed. Often, we sit around in a trailer waiting for the call, though, and depending on the movie, we may also spend a large part of our day putting on costumes and being made up by the make-up artists. It's a job that requires patience – and a fully charged smartphone! (Oh my goodness, what did extras do before smartphones? A book is fine for a trailer, but you can't hide it in your costume when you're in the middle of a scene!)

Obviously, I can't give you any of the details about my most recent job (top secret until it's released). I will just say that, although the majority of the movie is set in London, one scene was shot in a small town not far from New York. And that's where I came in. On a freezing cold winter day, dressed in just a light dress, with bare legs. (In the movie, it was late spring!) The main characters in the cast were played by really well-known British stars, but although some of them were in the U.S., none of them featured in my scene, unfortunately. So, no, I didn't meet any famous actors this time. Oh, and in case you're wondering, it wasn't the new Bond movie that's being released next month. Not this time …

43

UNIT 8

Sports and health

GRAMMAR: Tag questions

1 Choose the correct tag questions to complete the sentences.

1 She's really nice, *isn't it / isn't she / is she*?
2 You don't have Jamie's cell phone, *don't you / have you / do you*?
3 They were at the festival, *weren't they / didn't they / were they*?
4 Millie just got a new job, *doesn't she / didn't she / hasn't she*?
5 We're seeing you on Saturday, *aren't we / won't we / are we*?
6 Dan and Lucy are leaving, *aren't they / won't they / are they*?
7 It won't cause any problems, *won't it / does it / will it*?
8 Isabel speaks Spanish, *doesn't Isabel / doesn't she / does she*?
9 We should take a gift, *should we / shouldn't we / won't we*?
10 I can't call you at work, *will I / can I / can't I*?

2 Look at the tag questions. Then complete the sentences with the verbs in parentheses.

1 Ben _____ (go) to a gym in town, doesn't he?
2 Taylor _____ (come) in first in the race, didn't she?
3 They _____ (invite) Joe, have they?
4 You _____ (play) hockey, do you?
5 It _____ (be) an exciting game, won't it?
6 You _____ (bring) your phone, haven't you?
7 Tom _____ (be) at the game last night, was he?
8 We _____ (be) late, will we?
9 Antonio _____ (drive) us there, couldn't he?
10 They _____ (have to) pay for the service, should they?
11 You _____ (take) care of it, won't you?
12 He _____ (tell) Alia, did he?

VOCABULARY: Sports, places, and equipment

3 Complete the sentences with the words in the box.

| pool | ice skating | circuit | net | track and field | goal | bat | field |

1 She runs and jumps well, so she's really good at _____.
2 Halfway through the soccer game, he left the _____.
3 That's the _____ where Rachel swims each morning.
4 She kicked the ball well, but just missed the _____.
5 He hit the ball hard with his _____.
6 I love watching the cars race around the _____.
7 She jumped high and tried to hit the ball over the _____.
8 In winter, they go _____ on the frozen lake.

4 Read the definitions and complete the words.

1 This object is used for hitting a ball. It has a long handle and a round part. r___ ___ ___ ___ ___
2 This large, flat area is often covered with ice and is used for skating on. r___ ___ ___
3 You play this game with a brown ball that is the shape of an egg. f___ ___ ___ ___ ___ ___ ___
4 You wear these to protect your eyes in the water. g___ ___ ___ ___ ___ ___ ___
5 In this event, fast cars go around a road in the shape of a ring. a___ ___ ___ r___ ___ ___
6 An area for playing games like tennis, marked with lines. c___ ___ ___ ___
7 In this sport, you enter the water, usually with your head first. d___ ___ ___ ___ ___ ___
8 In this sport, you hit a small hard ball with a bat. b___ ___ ___ ___ ___ ___ ___ ___
9 This ring-shaped path is used for running around. t___ ___ ___ ___ ___

PRONUNCIATION: Intonation

5 ▶ 8.1 Listen to the sentences. Match them with a or b.

a asking a real question (intonation goes up)
b making a comment (intonation goes down)

1 They play tennis, don't they? _____
2 Alfonso doesn't eat meat, does he? _____
3 Laura wasn't at Amanda's house, was she? _____
4 You don't like swimming, do you? _____
5 John and Adrian aren't coming, are they? _____
6 You'll get there in time, won't you? _____

SKILLS 8B

LISTENING: Understanding facts and figures

1 ▶ 8.2 Daisy is asking her friend Luke about marathon running. Read the questions and circle the type of information you need to listen for. Then listen and answer the questions.

1 How long is a marathon in kilometers?
   date / length of time / distance / price / number
   Answer _____

2 How many marathons has Luke run?
   date / length of time / distance / price / number
   Answer _____

3 When did Luke run his first marathon?
   date / length of time / distance / price / number
   Answer _____

4 How long did his first marathon take?
   date / length of time / distance / price / number
   Answer _____

5 How long does it take Luke to run a marathon now?
   date / length of time / distance / price / number
   Answer _____

6 When is the Asheville, North Carolina Marathon?
   date / length of time / distance / price / number
   Answer _____

7 How long is it until the Asheville Marathon?
   date / length of time / distance / price / number
   Answer _____

8 When training for a marathon, by how much should you increase your distance each week?
   date / length of time / distance / price / number
   Answer _____

9 How much does the Boston Marathon cost runners?
   date / length of time / distance / price / number
   Answer _____

10 How many steps does the Great Wall Marathon have?
   date / length of time / distance / price / number
   Answer _____

2 ▶ 8.3 <u>Underline</u> the part or parts of the sentences where you expect the intonation to fall. Listen, check, and repeat.

1 Make sure you have days off so your muscles can recover.
2 The first marathon ever was in Athens.
3 Joe gets up at five every morning to have time to run.
4 I stopped training because I injured my leg.
5 Laura uses a pedometer to count her steps.
6 Swimming practice starts at eight this morning.
7 I run faster if I run with friends.
8 Take plenty of water in case you get thirsty.

3 Complete the words.

1 Jenny has been trying to eat more, but she is still u __ __ __ __ __ __ __ __ __.
2 Many illnesses are caused by people having an unhealthy l __ __ __ __ __ __ __ __.
3 Peter's on a d __ __ __ at the moment because he wants to lose weight for his wedding.
4 Make sure you eat a b __ __ __ __ __ __ __ diet with plenty of vegetables and fish.
5 I usually eat healthy food, but I have a few bad h __ __ __ __ __ __ like buying potato chips on my way back from work.
6 Tia finds that regular exercise helps her to get a good night's s __ __ __ __.
7 It's a good idea to do some e __ __ __ __ __ __ __ __ before you go on a skiing vacation.
8 Laurence is o __ __ __ __ __ __ __ __ __ because he eats a lot of cheese.
9 Tanya really got in s __ __ __ __ when she worked as a tennis coach.
10 It's easy to get s __ __ __ __ __ __ __ out if you don't have enough time to prepare for an important competition.

8C LANGUAGE

GRAMMAR: Modals of obligation and advice

1 Choose the correct options to complete the sentences.

1 You ___ come to my parents' house with me. I can go on my own.
   a can't   b shouldn't   c don't have to
2 If you're not there, they'll leave without you, so you ___ be late.
   a can't   b don't have to   c must
3 I'm a bit tired today. I ___ work eleven hours yesterday.
   a have to   b had to   c can
4 You ___ look at screens before bedtime as it stops you from sleeping.
   a have to   b don't have to   c shouldn't
5 I'm wondering what to do. Perhaps I ___ speak to Sarah.
   a can't   b have to   c should
6 If Lara is away next week, she will ___ cancel her doctor's appointment.
   a have to   b can   c should
7 I ___ remember Magda's birthday this year. Isn't she turning 40?
   a can't   b should   c have to
8 Do we ___ finish the report by Friday? There is still so much to do.
   a had to   b have to   c allowed to

2 Complete 1–6 with *should* or the correct form of *have to*. There may be more than one answer.

Raj	How are you doing with the packing? Have you asked Luke to bring some cooking equipment?
Naomi	No, not yet. He's still on the plane. I'll ¹___ speak to him later when he lands.
Raj	I hear it's going to be freezing cold this weekend, so we ²___ take the extra-warm sleeping bags.
Naomi	They're already in the car! By the way, be ready for an early start tomorrow morning! I know you hate ³___ get up early, but we're leaving at six.
Raj	Oh, really? Do we ⁴___ leave so early?
Naomi	Don't you remember last year? We ⁵___ sit in traffic for two hours because it was so busy.
Raj	You're right. I'd forgotten about that. I really ⁶___ get to bed early!

3 Complete the conversations with the correct form of *have to*, *can*, or *should*.

1 A Dan doesn't know about the problem yet.
   B He doesn't? Perhaps you ___ tell him at all.
2 A Would you like us to bring any food this evening?
   B Well, we'll have plenty, so you ___.
3 A We just missed the bus!
   B Oh, well. We'll just ___ get the next one.
4 A So does Sam know about the party?
   B Absolutely not! It's a surprise for his birthday, so you ___ tell him!
5 A See you at the airport at nine o'clock.
   B Great! And remember, this time you ___ bring your passport!
6 A Charlie always looks lonely. He doesn't seem to have many friends.
   B I think we ___ ask him to go to the movies with us?
7 A I don't feel so good. I think I'm getting a cold.
   B Well, perhaps you ___ go out tonight.
8 A Why were you at the meeting?
   B My boss wasn't able to attend, so I ___ go.
9 A There's a managers' meeting in Toronto next month, and I'd like Julia to attend.
   B Does she ___ go? She's very busy right now.
10 A Marco loves his summer job. He's working nights at a restaurant on the beach.
    B Sounds perfect for him. He ___ get up early!

PRONUNCIATION: Sentence stress

4 ▶ 8.4 Read the sentences and underline the verbs of obligation and advice you think will be stressed. Listen, check, and repeat.

1 You have to call your brother.
2 He should speak to James first.
3 You shouldn't work so hard.
4 I have to remember to take my phone.
5 She can't tell Alfonso.
6 You don't have to reserve.
7 Adam will have to call her and explain.
8 I guess I should complain.

SKILLS 8D

WRITING: Writing a report

HOW TO BE AN ACTIVE ADULT

(1) Most adults stay in shape / Most adults don't get enough exercise
It is recommended that all adults should do at least 150 minutes of moderate aerobic activity a week. However, 30% of adults exercise for less than 30 minutes per week.

(2) The benefits of exercise / Too much exercise can be bad for you
It is well known that physical activity has a number of positive results. It reduces the risk of many illnesses such as heart disease and even cancer. Moreover, exercise improves our mental health and can help us to lose weight.

(3) Practice a sport every day / Exercise a little every day
We all lead very busy lives, so it can be difficult to find enough time for exercise. I suggest having shorter periods of activity – perhaps ten minutes here and there throughout the day. In addition, you should try to incorporate exercise into your everyday activities. For example, you can walk up and down while you are on the phone, or why not use the stairs instead of taking the elevator?

(4) Spend less time working / Turn off your screens
Many of us spend far too much time sitting down, often in front of a screen. It is easy to spend the evening watching TV after a long day at work. In addition to this, spending time online can take up a lot of our day. All of this is time when we are hardly moving our bodies, so you should try to switch off and do something more active instead.

(5) Be active together / Get more exercise
Most things are more fun if you do them with someone else, and exercise is no exception. If you plan to go swimming with a friend, you are less likely to change your mind and stay at home. I would also recommend finding a physical activity that the whole family can enjoy – that way you can get in shape and spend quality time together, as well.

1. Read the report about exercise. Choose the best heading for each paragraph (1–5).

2. Complete the sentences with the words and phrases in the box and add commas where necessary. There may be more than one answer.

   > as well   as well as   in addition to this
   > in addition   moreover

   1. It can be difficult for some children to find time for sports _____ their homework and other activities.
   2. Too much time on a computer can make children get out of shape. _____ it can lead to sleep problems.
   3. Children who love swimming may enjoy other water sports _____.
   4. Bicycling is a great way for children to get in shape. _____ it is a great activity for families to do together.
   5. Many schools arrange after-school sports clubs. _____ you can often find local clubs that organize activities in the evenings or on the weekend.

3. Think of ways to encourage children to be more active. Complete the sentences with your ideas.

   1. To make sports more fun for your child, I would recommend doing some activities together.
   2. When you take your children swimming, remember to _____.
   3. If your child hates team sports, I suggest _____.
   4. If your child does not play many sports at school, I recommend _____.
   5. If your children do a lot of hard physical activity, remember to _____.
   6. To encourage your child to watch less TV, I suggest _____.

4. Write a report about encouraging children to be more active. Use ideas from exercises 2 and 3, as well as your own ideas.
   - Plan four or five section headings.
   - Include factual information.
   - Make recommendations using *suggest* or *recommend* + *-ing*, or *remember*.
   - Use the words and phrases from exercise 2 to add information.

8 REVIEW and PRACTICE

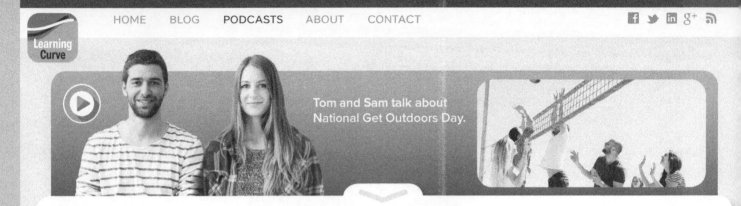

LISTENING

1 ▶ 8.5 Listen to the podcast and number a–f in the order that you hear them (1–6).

a Hugo's reasons for taking part in National Get Outdoors Day _____
b the advantages of getting exercise outdoors _____
c how Hugo plans to lose weight this time _____
d Tom's plans for National Get Outdoors Day _____
e Hugo's plans for National Get Outdoors Day _____
f what Hugo eats when he gets stressed out _____

2 ▶ 8.5 Listen again and choose the correct options to complete the sentences.

1 The main aim of National Get Outdoors Day is to encourage people to
  a go outside and enjoy nature.
  b go outside and do some physical activity.
  c spend some time with their friends outdoors.
2 Hugo has planned to
  a play volleyball and soccer.
  b play soccer and have lunch outside.
  c play volleyball and soccer and have lunch outside.
3 Hugo tells Sam and Tom that he is
  a slightly overweight.
  b very overweight.
  c not at all overweight.
4 Hugo says he is hoping to lose weight by
  a playing more soccer.
  b being more active.
  c eating less.
5 What example of a bad habit does Sam give?
  a driving instead of walking
  b eating chocolate
  c bicycling instead of walking
6 Sam says being outdoors makes her
  a eat less.
  b exercise more.
  c feel less stressed out.

READING

1 Read Taylor's blog on page 49 and choose the best summary.

a It is very important for people to get plenty of exercise every day.
b Some of the advice about exercise on the Internet is very strange.
c We should not give other people advice about how to exercise.

2 Are the sentences true (T), false (F), or doesn't say (DS)?

1 Taylor doesn't exercise every day. _____
2 She thinks we should all spend more time exercising. _____
3 She says that it is hard for busy people to find enough time to exercise. _____
4 She thinks it is a good idea to wear the same clothes to exercise and sleep in. _____
5 She always wears pajamas in bed. _____
6 She thinks it is a bad idea to exercise while waiting in line. _____
7 She thinks conversation might be difficult during a "sports date." _____
8 She recommends wearing red clothes while you are exercising. _____

3 Find words or phrases from the text that mean:

1 someone who helps you exercise
2 a reminder of the things you need to do
3 night clothes
4 get exercise
5 can't breathe easily
6 water produced by the skin

HOME BLOG PODCASTS ABOUT CONTACT

Guest blogger Taylor writes about advice on exercise.

EXERCISE MAD

You all know that I work as a personal trainer and that I'm crazy about yoga, so you might expect me to recommend getting some serious exercise every day. But you'd be wrong. Exercise is great – I'm a big fan – but most of us have a lot more going on in our lives than going to the gym, don't we?

In an ideal world, we'd all have an hour a day in which to get in shape. However, in the real world, 24 hours is often not enough time to work (or go to school), spend time with our family, and get eight hours' sleep. Some days, exercise just comes lower down the to-do list. And that's totally fine.

But that's clearly not how everyone feels. Lately, I've been reading some really strange advice on the Internet, given by people who take fitness very seriously. Some of it is so weird I feel the need to share it with you:

- *"You should wear your exercise clothes to bed. Then, you can get up and go for that early-morning run right away."* Sounds reasonable, doesn't it? No, it does not! The clothes that we exercise in are fitted and tight. And the clothes we sleep in are designed to be loose and cool and comfortable. You don't really want to sweat all night in your yoga pants, do you? Surely you'd rather get a good night's sleep in your pajamas, wouldn't you?

- *"While you're waiting in line, why not get a bit of exercise? Yes, folks, if you're standing in line at the supermarket checkout, and you have nothing to do, why not work out? If you're waiting at the airport for a delayed flight, why not get out your yoga mat?"* Because that will look really normal, won't it? And, what's more, if there's anyone within a couple of meters of you, with all that jumping around and waving of arms, it might even be dangerous!

- *"Make a sports date with your new girlfriend or boyfriend. A run or a session at the gym is a great way to get to know someone, isn't it?"* Especially when you're so out of breath that you can't even talk to the person! And, I'm sure you would agree, wouldn't you, that we all want to look our best when we go on a date – not red-faced and covered in sweat after half an hour at the gym!

- *"You should wear red when you exercise. This powerful color can give you extra energy while you try to get in shape."* Honestly, who writes this stuff? They can't really believe it, can they?

UNIT 9 Food

9A LANGUAGE

GRAMMAR: Uses of *like*

1 Complete the conversation with the words and phrases in the box.

> feel like   was it like   seems like
> would like   like   doesn't like   is like
> would you like

A We went to the new Italian restaurant in town last night.
B Oh, you did? What ¹_____?
A Great. I loved it. I really ²_____ Italian food – it's my favorite, and this was one of the best. You and Chris should go there sometime.
B I really ³_____ to go, but you know what Chris ⁴_____! He ⁵_____ any kind of Mediterranean food. In fact, he doesn't really like eating out at all.
A Oh no! That's such a shame!
B Yes, sometimes I ⁶_____ leaving him at home and going out with friends, instead.
A Well that ⁷_____ a great idea to me! ⁸_____ to come with us the next time we go? We'd be very happy to have you join us!

2 Use the prompts to write sentences with the correct use of *like*.

1 Molly/like/swimming. She's afraid of water.
   _____

2 I'm/teacher/but/like/be/writer.
   _____

3 what/the concert/like/last night?
   _____

4 you/like/go/movies/this evening?
   _____

5 My grandmother's great! I/want/like/her.
   _____

6 What is this meat? It/taste/like/chicken.
   _____

VOCABULARY: Food and cooking

3 Order the letters to make food words.

1 I didn't feel like cooking last night, so we got **koteatu** _____ pizza for dinner.
2 Supermarket cakes are never as nice as **ehomedam** _____ ones.
3 We dipped pieces of bread in a big pot of **teldem** _____ cheese.
4 It was a simple meal – a piece of **lerdigl** _____ fish on rice.
5 Would you like some **tedrag** _____ cheese on your pasta?
6 I sometimes have a **lobied** _____ egg and toast for breakfast.
7 They sell bread and cakes and other **kabde** _____ products.
8 Serve the dish with **lisdec** _____ tomatoes on top.

4 Complete the sentences with food words.

1 S_____h are small sea creatures with hard coverings that you can eat.
2 O_____ o_____ is often used for salad dressings, sometimes with vinegar or lemon juice.
3 An a_____o has dark green skin, a large stone, and green flesh that is soft and not sweet.
4 A s_____ is a thick flat piece of meat, usually from a cow.
5 A_____s is a green vegetable with long, thin stems.
6 G_____ is white and grows under the ground. It has a very strong taste!
7 A z_____i is long and usually has dark green skin. It has seeds and contains a lot of water.
8 A l_____ is a small fruit like a lemon with green skin and sour juice.

PRONUNCIATION: /dʒ/ sound

5 ▶9.1 Listen to the sentences. Are *did you* and *would you* pronounced with /dy/ or /dʒ/ sounds? Listen again and repeat.

1	What would you like to do now?	/dy/	/dʒ/
2	What did you like doing in the evenings?	/dy/	/dʒ/
3	Would you like to come with us?	/dy/	/dʒ/
4	Would you like to dance?	/dy/	/dʒ/
5	What would you like for lunch?	/dy/	/dʒ/
6	Where did you go on vacation?	/dy/	/dʒ/
7	When did you go?	/dy/	/dʒ/
8	Where did you meet?	/dy/	/dʒ/

SKILLS 9B

READING: Reading for detail

Can you have a healthy diet on a low budget?
Yes, says Bonnie Naylor, if you follow these tips.

A Eat before you shop
Going to the supermarket on an empty stomach is a recipe for over spending! You simply won't be able to resist that extra bar of chocolate or that yummy-looking piece of cheese. So eat first and go with a list – having ¹one and sticking to it is a great way to avoid waste.

B Stay local
Remember, too, that if something is grown in a far-away country, you are paying for transportation as well as the food itself. Avocados may be cheap in Mexico, but in London, they're still a bit of a luxury. And why buy carrots from halfway around the world when ²ones from your own country are cheaper and taste just the same?

C A new best friend!
When you're on a tight budget, lentils are your best friend! Low in calories, packed with fiber, vitamins, and minerals – what's not to like? Look online for tasty lentil recipes – there are some great ³ones around. Try other legumes, too – use chickpeas to replace half the chicken in a curry, for example. You'll save money, and it will taste just as good.

D Go wild (well, a bit!)
I'm not suggesting you go out hunting a deer (although apparently "survival" vacations where participants have to kill and prepare any meat they eat are becoming increasingly popular with urban office workers). Foraging is the name of the game – in the woods for mushrooms, nuts, and berries,

or on the seashore for shellfish or even edible seaweed. A word of warning though – you need to educate yourself first! The right kind of mushroom is about the most delicious thing you can imagine; the wrong ⁴one could kill you.

E Beware the BOGOF!
Look out for special offers of course, but they need to be the right ⁵ones. Don't be tempted by "Buy One Get One Free" offers unless they're for something you actually want – can you really eat two very ripe pineapples within 24 hours? A better bet is to go to the market near the end of the day.

---

1 Read the text quickly then underline the key words in the questions in exercise 2. Write A–E for the paragraph where you think you will find the answer.

1 ____   5 ____
2 ____   6 ____
3 ____   7 ____
4 ____

2 Read the text again and choose the correct options.

1 Why is it a bad idea to shop when you are hungry?
  a You will need to buy extra food to fill up.
  b You will want to buy things that you do not need.
  c You will do your shopping too quickly and make bad choices.

2 How can you avoid buying things you don't need?
  a Stop buying things like chocolate and cheese.
  b Be careful not to buy food you will waste.
  c Write down everything you want to buy.

3 Why are avocados expensive in London?
  a It costs a lot to get them to the UK.
  b They are rare in UK stores.
  c Not enough people want to buy them.

4 What reasons does the article give for buying lentils?
  a They are cheap, healthy, and don't make you fat.
  b They taste good and are filling.
  c You can use them instead of meat.

5 What kind of people go on survival vacations?
  a People who want to get free meat.
  b People who know a lot about collecting food from the wild.
  c People who usually live in cities and work in offices.

6 Why can it be dangerous to collect food from the countryside?
  a It's not easy to know which seaweed you can eat.
  b You could easily get lost.
  c Some plants are poisonous.

7 Why do you need to be careful with special offers?
  a The quality of the food may not be very high.
  b They may encourage you to buy more than you can use.
  c The food may sometimes be rotten.

3 Find the five examples of *one* or *ones* in the text. Write the nouns that they substitute.

1 _____   4 _____
2 _____   5 _____
3 _____

9C LANGUAGE

GRAMMAR: -ing forms and infinitives

1 Complete the sentences with the correct form of the verbs in parentheses.

1 It's cheaper (travel) _____ coach class on the train.
2 Is Phil good at (play) _____ the piano?
3 Lara was looking forward to (visit) _____ her cousin.
4 I'll call Joe when we've finished (eat) _____ dinner.
5 Anna plans to go to Australia (do) _____ some sightseeing.
6 I don't mind (pay) _____ for your train ticket.
7 I'm not sure what time you want (leave) _____ this evening?
8 Allan asked me (carry) _____ his suitcase.
9 Sylvia doesn't feel like (go out) _____. She has a bad headache.
10 (Run) _____ is really hard for me. I have bad knees.

2 Complete the sentences with the correct form of the verbs in the box.

| forget   meet   not wake   come   find   not have |
| not make   fly   swim   invite   see   call |

1 We looked everywhere _____ the perfect present for Valeria.
2 I'm nervous about the trip abroad because I'm scared of _____.
3 Alice was asleep, and we decided _____ her.
4 _____ is a great form of exercise.
5 I'm thinking of _____ Nigel to my birthday party.
6 I forgot my phone. I hate _____ it with me.
7 Mavis is in such good shape it's easy _____ that she's almost 90.
8 We told the children _____ too much noise.
9 _____ new people is exciting.
10 We asked her to join us in the park, but she refused _____.
11 The doctor told Graham _____ him on his cell-phone number.
12 I recommend _____ the city at night. The lights are amazing.

VOCABULARY: Eating out

3 Complete 1–3 with the words in the box.

| bowl   fork   knife   medium   pepper |
| plate   rare   salt   spoon   vinegar |
| well-done |

1 things that add flavor to food
_____   _____   _____

2 things used for serving and eating food
_____   _____   _____
_____   _____

3 ways to describe how long meat is cooked for
_____   _____   _____

4 Complete the words.

1 It's getting late. Let's ask the waiter for the _____k and pay.
2 I like quiet restaurants, but my boyfriend prefers somewhere with a more lively a_____e.
3 Shrimp curry sounds nice. I think I'll _____r that.
4 He finished eating and wiped his mouth with a _____in.
5 It's a popular restaurant – I think we should _____e a table.
6 I was so embarrassed when I spilt coffee all over the clean white _____e_____h!
7 The waiter was very helpful, so we left him a big _____p.
8 Our meal took two hours to come. The _____e was so slow.

PRONUNCIATION: -ing

5 ▶ 9.2 Listen to the sentences. Are the -ing syllables pronounced as /ɪŋ/ or /ɪn/? Listen again and repeat.

1 Reading is my main hobby.	/ɪŋ/	/ɪn/
2 I really miss talking to Jenny.	/ɪŋ/	/ɪn/
3 We went skiing in Austria.	/ɪŋ/	/ɪn/
4 I recommend reserving a table.	/ɪŋ/	/ɪn/
5 I'm playing tennis with Sam.	/ɪŋ/	/ɪn/
6 I love having friends over for a meal.	/ɪŋ/	/ɪn/

SKILLS 9D

SPEAKING: Making and responding to suggestions

1 ▶ 9.3 Listen to the conversations between Kris, Hannah, and Aidan. Check (✓) the correct name or names.

	Kris	Hannah	Aidan
1 Who suggests going for pizza?			
2 Who has already had pizza today?			
3 Who has never been to the Mexican restaurant before?			
4 Who can't eat shrimp?			
5 Who asks for an opinion about the zucchini?			
6 Who enjoyed the zucchini?			
7 Who wanted to leave the biggest tip?			
8 Who tried to persuade Kris to leave a bigger tip?			
9 Who liked the waitress?			
10 Who changed his or her mind about the tip?			

2 ▶ 9.3 Listen again and check (✓) the phrases you hear. Write M if they are for making a suggestion, P for responding positively, and N for responding negatively.

1 Should we … ____
2 That sounds great. ____
3 Well, I'm not sure. ____
4 To be honest, I'd rather … ____
5 Of course. ____
6 Great idea! ____
7 I suggest we … ____
8 Yes, let's. ____
9 I won't have any, if that's OK. ____
10 Why don't you … ? ____
11 I was wondering if we could … ____
12 Can't we …, instead? ____

3 Use your own ideas and some of the phrases in exercise 2 to complete these conversations.

1 Two friends are deciding what to do on a day off.
   A (Make a suggestion) _____
   B (Give a negative response and suggest something different) _____
   A (Try to persuade B to change his/her mind)
   _____
   B (Agree to A's suggestion) _____

2 Two friends are discussing a movie they have both seen.
   A (Ask for B's opinion on the movie)
   _____
   B (Give an opinion) _____
   A (Disagree with B's opinion and give reasons)
   _____
   B (Say you do not agree with A)
   _____

9 REVIEW and PRACTICE

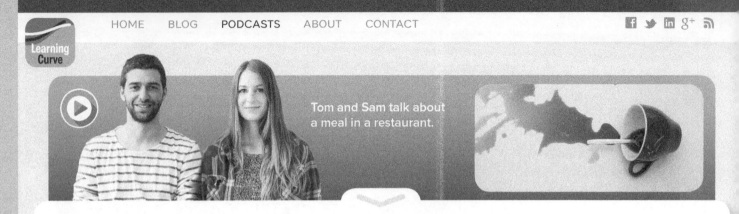

HOME   BLOG   **PODCASTS**   ABOUT   CONTACT

Tom and Sam talk about a meal in a restaurant.

LISTENING

1 ▶ 9.4 Listen to the podcast and number a–f in the order that they are mentioned (1–6).

a an accident involving a cup of coffee ____
b how long the meat had been cooked ____
c an argument about the table they had reserved ____
d the table that Gabriel and his girlfriend were given ____
e the appearance of the restaurant ____
f how long they had to wait for their food ____

2 ▶ 9.4 Listen again and complete the sentences with one or two words.

1 Sam reminded Tom that he had some _____ while he was working as a waiter.
2 The waiter said that Gabriel had asked for a table for _____ people.
3 Gabriel asked for a table by _____.
4 Gabriel and his girlfriend were given a table near the _____ the restaurant.
5 Gabriel said that the waiter was _____ to them.
6 Their food took a long time to _____.
7 Gabriel's girlfriend ordered a rare _____.
8 The service was not very good, so Gabriel did not leave _____.

READING

1 Read Jack's blog on page 55 and check (✓) the things he mentions.

a his views on different diets, such as vegetarianism and veganism ____
b how many dishes he is prepared to cook ____
c the kind of food he especially likes eating ____
d the fact that one of his friends is trying to lose weight ____
e the place where he is going to have his dinner party ____

2 Does Jack say these things in his blog? Circle Yes (Y) or No (N).

1 He is worried that he is getting old. Y / N
2 He wants to celebrate other things in addition to his birthday. Y / N
3 Two of his guests have decided to get married. Y / N
4 Five of his guests do not eat meat. Y / N
5 Two of his guests have problems with their health when they eat certain foods. Y / N
6 One of his guests has recently changed his/her diet. Y / N
7 Apart from the engaged couple, none of his guests know each other. Y / N
8 The menus have to include suggestions for drinks. Y / N
9 There will be rewards for the best menus. Y / N
10 He is hoping that his readers will create different and surprising menus. Y / N

3 Make a list of all the food items mentioned in the text.

REVIEW and PRACTICE 9

HOME BLOG PODCASTS ABOUT CONTACT

Guest blogger Jack writes about a special dinner party.

Cooking challenge

Cooking for friends is one of life's great pleasures. (I know, I would say that – I'm a chef!) So, to celebrate my birthday this year – the big three-oh – I've decided to make dinner for ten of my closest friends. I'd like to make this a really special evening, for several reasons.

One of my guests has just returned from three years in Australia, two other friends have recently gotten engaged and another – my oldest and dearest friend – has just been promoted at work. Life is good, and we're in the mood for celebrating! However, this is a slightly different kind of dinner party, because my *fabulous* friends have very particular (and very varied) food requirements. They are as follows:

- **Guest no. 1** is a strict vegetarian, but hates eating garlic. (I mean, really hates it and can taste it in the *tiniest* quantities!)

- **Guest no. 2** is also a vegetarian, but can't eat nuts of any kind. They make her sick. Oh, and she *really* doesn't like avocados. (How can anyone not like avocados?)

- **Guest no. 3** has recently turned vegan (so absolutely no animal products, including milk, eggs, yogurt, etc.) Also, he's not fond of soy sauce or other soya products.

- **Guest no. 4** doesn't eat meat, but is fine with fish (but not shellfish).

- **Guest no. 5** is on a diet so, if possible, would like to avoid cheese, desserts, and fried foods.

- **Guest no. 6** is allergic to citrus fruit, so absolutely no oranges, lemons or limes.

- **Guest no. 7** likes meat and pretty much nothing else. (Strangely, his best friend is guest no. 3!)

- **Guests 8, 9, 10** eat everything, in large quantities!

So, readers, I've decided to give you a challenge! Now that you've been presented with this long list of requirements and preferences, what would your menu look like? It has to include a starter, a main course, and a dessert. Guests will serve themselves from dishes set on the table. I'm happy to cook two dishes for each course – perhaps three for the main course – in order to provide options that everyone can enjoy.

Oh, and the first prize is dinner for four at The Goode Food Restaurant at any time this year. The second prize is dinner for two! There'll be extra points for original and unusual ideas! Get busy planning your menus, folks!

UNIT 10 Right and wrong

10A LANGUAGE

GRAMMAR: Reported speech

1 Choose the correct options to complete the sentences.

1 "I can't swim." Max told me he *won't be able to / couldn't / cannot* swim.
2 "I'll give you $10." Carrie said she would give *her / you / me* $10.
3 "Do you like running?" Gary asked me *if I liked / did I like / if I had liked* running.
4 "What have you done with the money?" They asked me what *did I do / had I done / I had done* with the money.
5 "James is broke." Dan *told me / told to me / told* that James was broke.
6 "You should resign." Milo said that I *should resign / should have resigned / had resigned*.
7 "I'm working hard." Juliet said that she *worked / was working / had worked* hard.
8 "You could try calling." He said that I *could have tried / could try / try* calling.

2 Read the things that your friend said. Then, complete the reported speech sentences with the correct information.

- "I'm feeling nervous about my exam."
- "I saw Mr. Jones last week."
- "Have you visited Ged recently?"
- "I can't remember Maria's address."
- "Why did you go to Paris?"
- "Are you happy in college?"

1 **A** Is she ready for her exam?
   B I'm not sure. She said she _____ nervous about it.
2 **A** Did she mention Mr. Jones?
   B Yes, she said she _____ last week.
3 **A** Did she ask you anything about Ged?
   B Yes, she asked me _____ him recently.
4 **A** Did she give you Maria's address?
   B No, she said she _____ it.
5 **A** Did she ask you about Paris?
   B Yes, she asked me why I _____ there.
6 **A** Did she ask you about college?
   B Yes, she asked me _____ happy.

VOCABULARY: Crime

3 Read the statements and check (✓) True or False.

		True	False
1	A mugging usually takes place in someone's home.		
2	People sometimes have to pay a fine for a crime that is not very serious.		
3	A burglar usually steals money from a bank.		
4	If something is against the law, you may be punished if you do it.		
5	"Theft" is a general word for the crime of stealing things.		
6	Someone who has been killed is called a murderer.		
7	It is possible to mug someone without that person realizing a crime has taken place.		
8	A thief is someone who has taken something that belongs to someone else.		

4 Complete the newspaper articles with crime words.

Police are looking for a man after a ¹b_____ at the home of a wealthy city art dealer last week. He ²b_____ into the house through a back window while the owner was out and ³s_____ jewelry and paintings worth several thousand dollars. The ⁴s_____, described by a ⁵w_____ who saw him running to a getaway car, is a slim man with dark hair.

A woman has appeared in ⁶c_____, accused of ⁷m_____ after a body was discovered in a house in Brooklyn. Police ⁸a_____ her after finding photographs of the ⁹v_____ in her apartment. If she is found guilty, she is likely to spend years in ¹⁰p_____.

PRONUNCIATION: Sentence stress

5 ▶ 10.1 Listen to the sentences. Are the underlined words stressed (S) or unstressed (U)? Listen again and repeat.

1 Liam said <u>that</u> he was tired. _____
2 I asked them <u>why</u> they were laughing. _____
3 Hannah asked <u>if</u> I wanted a drink. _____
4 Tom asked me <u>where</u> to go. _____
5 Petra asked me <u>who</u> I'd told. _____
6 They told her <u>why</u> they were angry. _____

SKILLS 10B

LISTENING: Listening in detail

1 ▶10.2 Alex and Lucy are talking about crimes. Underline the key words in the questions and options. Then listen and choose the correct options.

1 Why isn't Lucy feeling very happy?
   a Thieves stole things from her house.
   b Someone damaged the glass in her back door.
   c Burglars came into her house and woke her up.
2 What was Lucy doing while the incident was happening?
   a She was walking around upstairs.
   b She was listening to the people downstairs.
   c She was in bed.
3 What was taken from Lucy's house?
   a Her watch, laptop, phone, and car keys.
   b James's watch, laptop, phone, and car keys.
   c James's watch and laptop, Lucy's phone, and the car keys.
4 What happened to Alex's neighbor, Karen?
   a She had a nightmare.
   b She was robbed on the street.
   c A burglar stole her necklace.
5 Why was Karen's necklace special?
   a Her husband gave it to her when they got married.
   b It was worth a lot of money.
   c It was a birthday present from her husband.
6 Who saw what happened to Karen?
   a a man riding a bike
   b someone in a car
   c a witness walking nearby
7 What happened to the criminal Alex is telling Lucy about?
   a He was arrested and gave the necklace back.
   b He was arrested and sent to prison.
   c He was arrested and has to go to court.
8 Lucy would feel better if
   a the burglars hadn't stolen her phone.
   b the police had found her car.
   c the burglars had been arrested.

2 ▶10.2 Choose the correct options to complete these sentences. Listen again if you need to.

1 The glass in Lucy's back door *was / wasn't* broken by the burglars.
2 The burglars only stole things from *upstairs / downstairs*.
3 The thieves stole Lucy's *phone / laptop*.
4 Alex's neighbor was robbed by a *burglar / mugger*.
5 Karen's necklace was a *birthday / wedding* present.
6 The attack on Karen was seen by a witness who was *walking / driving* by.
7 Alex doesn't know if Karen's attacker will go to *prison / court*.
8 Lucy can't *sleep / relax* in her house because of the burglary.

3 ▶10.3 Find words that end with /t/ and /d/ sounds in sentences 1–6. Write _ if they are linked to the next sound and circle them if they are not pronounced. Listen, check, and repeat.

1 My neighbor was mugged at three o'clock in the afternoon.
2 It had been her wedding present from her husband.
3 Someone driving by saw what was happening.
4 He has to go to court next week.
5 It happened so fast there was nothing she could do.
6 The man was arrested and sent to prison.

4 Complete the sentences with nouns made from the verbs in the box. There are three extra verbs.

> achieve review argue educate disappoint
> inform imagine decide organize govern
> confuse connect protect

1 There was some _____ about the date of the meeting: Rob thought it was the 2nd, but Emma said it was the 4th.
2 They planted a row of trees to provide some _____ from the strong winds.
3 Maria continued her _____ at an art college in Japan.
4 There is a strong _____ between physical and emotional health.
5 The company was losing money, so we made the _____ to close it.
6 Winning an Oscar is an incredible _____.
7 Hans went online to find _____ about careers in fashion.
8 The children's stories showed a lot of _____.
9 We could see Olga's _____ when she failed to win the competition.
10 Seb and Georgie were having an _____ about who should wash the dishes.

10C LANGUAGE

GRAMMAR: Second conditional, *would*, *could*, and *might*

1 Complete the sentences with the first or second conditional form of the verbs in parentheses.

1. If Sima _____ (start) a new hobby, she wouldn't be so bored.
2. I'm sure Yvette _____ (help) with the housework if Robin asked her to.
3. If Kazuo _____ (sell) all his paintings, he'd be able to buy a motorcycle.
4. We can go skiing if it _____ (snow).
5. If Max _____ (bring) some money, we can buy ice cream.
6. We _____ (have) a lot of problems if the machine broke.
7. If Alicia _____ (sell) her apartment, she won't have anywhere to live.
8. Pavel _____ (cook) dinner if you ask him to.

2 Complete the conversation with the correct form of the verbs in the box.

| be able | pay | not criticize | not waste |
| be | cook | not spend | not be | have | ride |

Leo I wish you were coming on vacation with us, Greta. It would be much more fun if you ¹_____ there.

Greta I'd come if I ²_____ more money, but I can't afford it.

Leo You'd be able to afford it if you ³_____ so much on clothes.

Greta It's my job that's the problem, not my clothes! If my employer ⁴_____ me more, it ⁵_____ so difficult to save money.

Leo You could save more if you ⁶_____ your own meals instead of eating out all the time.

Greta But you know I hate cooking!

Leo Or if you ⁷_____ your bike, instead of taking cabs everywhere.

Greta And you know I don't like bike riding, either.

Leo All I'm saying is that if you ⁸_____ so much money, you ⁹_____ to come on vacation with us.

Greta Well I might try a bit harder if you ¹⁰_____ me so much!

3 Complete the conversations with second conditional sentences. Use the underlined verbs and the verbs in parentheses.

1. **A** Should we take a cab?
   B No, if we _____ a cab, it _____ (be) too expensive.
2. **A** Is your little brother coming to the party?
   B No, if he _____, I _____ (have to) look after him the whole time.
3. **A** Are you going to take the bus?
   B No, if I _____ the bus, I _____ (not arrive) in time.
4. **A** Should we go swimming?
   B No, if we _____ swimming, we _____ (miss) the soccer game on TV.
5. **A** Is Carla going to enter the competition?
   B No, she knows she _____ (not win) if she _____ it.
6. **A** Should we ask Bernie to come to the movies with us?
   B No, even if we _____ him, he _____ (not come).
7. **A** Are you going to buy that car you told me about?
   B No, I _____ (not have) any money left if I _____ it.
8. **A** Do you think we should tell Anna what Dan said?
   B No, if we _____ her, she _____ (be) very upset.

PRONUNCIATION: Conditionals

4 ▶ 10.4 Listen to the sentences. Write 1 for first conditionals and 2 for second conditionals. Listen again, check, and repeat.

1. ____
2. ____
3. ____
4. ____
5. ____
6. ____
7. ____
8. ____

WRITING: Writing a for-and-against essay

ONLY DANGEROUS CRIMINALS SHOULD GO TO PRISON. DISCUSS.

(A) However, one disadvantage is the cost. ¹_____ Sending people to prison can also have a very bad effect on their families, particularly if they have children. Moreover, prison can sometimes make people more likely to commit crimes in the future because they are influenced by other criminals that they meet there.

(B) Many countries have problems with their prison systems, and one of the major ones is that the prisons are often too full. ²_____ As a result, the prisoners do not have the chance to study or to gain work experience, which might help them lead better lives in the future. Therefore, some people think we should keep criminals who are not dangerous out of prisons and punish them in a different way.

(C) To sum up, I believe that we should only send people to prison if they are really dangerous. ³_____ However, I believe that we should find better methods of punishment, including ones that could have advantages for our society.

(D) The main advantage of sending criminals to prison is that it sends a clear message to society: if you commit a crime, you will be punished. ⁴_____ In addition, some crimes (for example, not paying large amounts of taxes) are not violent, but they are still very serious, and some people argue that people who commit these crimes should go to prison.

1 Read the for-and-against essay and number paragraphs A–D in the correct order 1–4.

1 ____   2 ____   3 ____   4 ____

2 Fill in blanks 1–4 in the essay with sentences a–f. There are two extra sentences.

a This does not mean that other criminals should not be punished.
b When this happens, staff cannot control the prisoners, and they spend most of their time in their cells.
c Children suffer when their parents are sent to prison.
d It is very expensive to keep someone in prison – as much as $60,000 a year in some states.
e I believe that anyone who commits murder should go to prison for life.
f Freedom is important to everyone and, if you know you could lose it, you might not commit a crime.

3 "It is impossible to be happy if you are poor. Discuss." Are these topic sentences arguments for (F) or against (A) the essay title?

1 The main advantage of having plenty of money is that it makes life less stressful. ____
2 To sum up, the love of your friends and family is the only thing that can really make you happy. ____
3 On the other hand, if you do not have much money, you will not have the chance to do as many interesting things in life. ____
4 However, one disadvantage of having a lot of money is that it can be difficult to know who your real friends are. ____
5 To sum up, happiness is difficult to achieve if you are always worrying about how to pay for the things you need. ____
6 On the one hand, it is certainly possible to have a lot of fun without spending much money. ____

4 Use your own ideas to complete topic sentences for the two essays.

1 "Cigarettes should be illegal. Discuss."
  a The main advantage of _____
  b However, one disadvantage _____
  c To sum up, _____

2 "Everyone should have the chance to go to college. Discuss."
  a On the one hand, _____
  b On the other hand, _____
  c To sum up, _____

5 Choose an essay title from exercise 3 or 4. Write a for-and-against essay.
- Write four paragraphs.
- Start each paragraph with a topic sentence, using ideas from exercise 3.
- Use a formal style.

10 REVIEW and PRACTICE

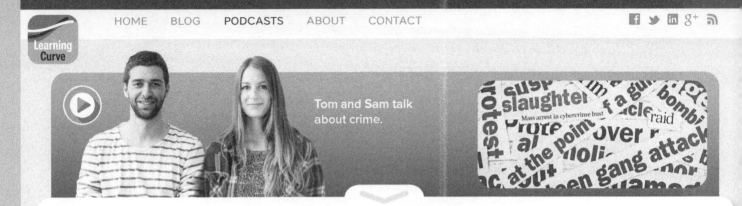

LISTENING

1 ▶ 10.5 Listen to the podcast and check (✓) the words that you hear.

a thieves
b steal
c victim
d arrest
e theft
f murders
g prison
h mugging
i burglaries
j robbery

2 ▶ 10.5 Listen again. Are the sentences true (T), false (F), or doesn't say (DS)?

1 Tom thinks that people's behavior is better these days.
2 Most people believe that we live in a better society than in the past.
3 Michael says that his family and friends are kind, honest people.
4 Thieves do not usually use the Internet to commit crime.
5 Tom has been a victim of online theft.
6 According to Michael, mugging is not a very serious crime.
7 In the area where Michael lives, there were more burglaries last year.
8 Michael's house was burglarized last year.

READING

1 Read Marc's blog on page 61 and check (✓) the things it says about the robber.

a He put pictures of himself with stolen money on Facebook.
b He stole a car after he robbed a Chase bank.
c He told friends about his plan to commit the crime before he did it.
d He used a different name on social media.
e He always used a gun when he robbed banks.

2 Choose the correct options to complete the sentences.

1 Marc admits that he does not know a lot about
  a social media.
  b movies.
  c criminals.
2 Using social media, Jesse Hippolite told his friends that he
  a had robbed a bank in New York.
  b planned to rob a bank in New York.
  c had robbed lots of banks in New York.
3 Someone helped the police by giving them information about Hippolite's
  a car.
  b social media account.
  c friends.
4 Hippolite's car
  a had been parked outside a bank that had been robbed.
  b had been parked outside many banks that had been robbed.
  c was in a picture he had posted on social media.
5 Willie Sutton
  a escaped from prison several times.
  b went to prison for 40 years.
  c was never sent to prison for his crimes.
6 Marc says the police believe Hippolite committed
  a three robberies.
  b sixteen robberies.
  c nineteen robberies.

HOME BLOG PODCASTS ABOUT CONTACT

Guest blogger Marc writes about an unfortunate criminal.

THE WORST CRIMINAL?

You know I like to use this blog to pass on stories that involve social media, especially ones that relate specifically to New York. Well, today I have an incredible one for you about a not-so-clever criminal called Jesse Hippolite.

Now, I'm no expert on criminal behavior, and perhaps I've watched a few too many gangster movies, but I'd always assumed that robbery was something that people did secretly. (You know, to avoid being arrested?) But this guy, who has apparently been responsible for robbing a large number of banks in the New York area, liked to do things differently. Last July, the 24-year-old bank robber told his friends on Facebook that he was going to rob a bank. He posted, "I Gotta Get that $$$$$ Man!!!!" on the social media site just an hour before he robbed a Chase bank in Brooklyn, New York. The young robber had also said on Facebook that crime "paid his bills," as well as posting several photographs of himself counting $100 bills for the camera.

And how was he found? Well, a witness to one of his robberies had written down Hippolite's license plate number and handed it to the police. So when the police were given his number, they used their CCTV camera system to check where his car had been parked during the previous weeks. It turned out that the car had been very near the scene of no less than nineteen different bank robberies. The police then examined the suspect's social media account (something the police often do now, apparently), and that told them all they needed to know.

The young criminal used the name Willie Sutton Jr. on his Facebook profile, the famous bank robber who, during his 40-year "career" from the 1920s to the 1950s, stole $2 million.

He spent over half of his life in prison, escaping no less than three times with the use of clever disguises.

Interestingly, Hippolite never used a gun in his robberies, preferring instead to hand over handwritten notes to bank staff that threatened: "GIVE ME ALL THE MONEY!!! $100s, $50s, $20s ONLY."

Hippolite, who was charged with committing three robberies and is a suspect in a further sixteen, admitted in court that he had carried out these crimes. He now faces a possible 60-year prison sentence. Should be plenty of time to regret his actions – and his stupidity!

UNIT 11 The natural world

11A LANGUAGE

GRAMMAR: Articles

1 Match the two parts of the sentences.

1 I think it's a _____
2 Luis Sylva is the _____
3 Ava and I met a _____
4 Danny and I watched an _____
5 You can't look at the _____
6 We can't just stay at _____
7 I love all his films, but this is the _____
8 We're excited because we're off to _____
9 My sister has always loved _____
10 On the way there, we flew over the _____

a amazing documentary about space.
b home all day!
c animals.
d Paris next week.
e Atlantic Ocean.
f very interesting woman at Lara's house.
g sun directly.
h really fascinating and original movie.
i best one of all.
j guy who we spoke to earlier.

2 Complete the sentences with the correct article or no article (–).

1 Sophie has always been terrified of _____ spiders.
2 He's studying Spanish, but _____ teacher's not very good.
3 I've always found history _____ really fascinating subject.
4 We're not sure what her job is. Perhaps she's _____ salesclerk.
5 Do you prefer _____ dogs or _____ cats?
6 It was a very beautiful hotel, but _____ service there was terrible.
7 What was _____ first country you ever visited?
8 He usually goes to _____ work around eight o'clock.
9 I have to admire _____ doctors. They do such a difficult job.
10 How many times _____ week do you cook at home?

VOCABULARY: The natural world

3 Complete the sentences with the words in the box.

| hail | hurricane | rainbow | tornado | monsoon |
| sea | icebergs | earthquake | flood | hill |

1 When the ground started to shake, I knew it was a(n) _____
2 There was a (n) _____ downtown after the banks of the local river burst.
3 We thought it was snow, but then realized it was _____.
4 Let's climb up the _____ to see the view over the town.
5 The _____ lasted almost two weeks, with winds reaching speeds of 180 miles an hour.
6 Melting _____ in these regions are causing sea levels to rise.
7 Look at that fantastic _____ in the sky!
8 Do you prefer the _____ or swimming pools?
9 I was there during the _____ season, so it was very wet.
10 They could see the _____ approaching – a spinning column of air.

4 Complete the words.

1 They're staying at a hotel on the c_____ of Thailand.
2 The Amazon Rainforest is a j_____ where more than 1,300 kinds of birds live.
3 Mount Vesuvius is an active v_____ in southern Italy. It last erupted in 1944.
4 Many of the trees in this f_____ have been cut down for fuel and building materials.
5 The world's largest hot d_____ is the Sahara in Africa.
6 If all the world's g_____ melted, sea levels would rise by about 70 meters.
7 She used to keep the horse in a f_____ behind her house.
8 Last night's huge s_____ brought wind and rain and destroyed many houses.

PRONUNCIATION: the

5 ▶ 11.1 Read the sentences. Is *the* pronounced /ðə/ or /ðiː/? Listen, check, and repeat.

1	They live in the Arctic.	/ðə/	/ðiː/
2	We made our way through the jungle.	/ðə/	/ðiː/
3	The icebergs are surrounded by fog.	/ðə/	/ðiː/
4	Have you seen the rainbow?	/ðə/	/ðiː/
5	We swam in the ocean.	/ðə/	/ðiː/
6	The earthquake destroyed a lot of buildings.	/ðə/	/ðiː/
7	Why don't you drive along the coast?	/ðə/	/ðiː/
8	Is the volcano still active?	/ðə/	/ðiː/

SKILLS 11B

READING: Understanding the writer's purpose

IF YOU CAN'T STAND THE HEAT ...

When we think of sunshine, happy scenes of vacations and beaches usually spring to mind. ¹But what about places like Death Valley in California or the Sahara Desert? Here, the heat is far from being pleasant – in fact, it's downright dangerous.

²Our bodies function within a fairly narrow temperature range, and conditions that cause a rise in that temperature can be extremely serious. People suffering from heatstroke lose the ability to regulate their temperature. ³This can lead to a range of symptoms from headaches and dizziness to heart and brain problems and sometimes death, all within an alarmingly short period of time.

Even people who have lived all their lives in hot countries can be affected. ⁴In 2015, over 1,300 people died during a heatwave in Karachi. With temperatures of over 40°C, hospitals were totally overwhelmed by the number of people suffering from heat-related illnesses. Interestingly, scientists have discovered that around half of the Aboriginal people in Western Australia have a gene that helps them survive at higher temperatures. It is not yet known why people in other hot climates have not evolved in the same way.

Despite the great heat, some people are attracted to the idea of traveling in extremely hot places like deserts. ⁵For such a trip, the most important thing is to take more water than you think you could possibly need. ⁶In addition to being extremely hot, deserts can also be very tricky to navigate, with sand and dunes stretching for miles in every direction, and there are many cases of people getting lost in them with fatal results.

---

1 Read the text and choose the correct options, according to the information given.

1 Why isn't sunshine always a good thing?
  a If you're not on vacation, it can be unpleasant.
  b Some types of heat are especially bad.
  c Too much heat can harm you.

2 Are our bodies well adapted for heat and cold?
  a No, we can only deal with small changes in temperature.
  b Yes, if we take care to regulate our temperature.
  c No, our bodies need to stay at the same temperature.

3 Do people often die when they get heatstroke?
  a No, most people recover pretty quickly.
  b Not everyone – some people have more minor symptoms.
  c Yes, and it happens pretty quickly.

4 What is unusual about some Aboriginal people?
  a They have developed to function better than most people in hot weather.
  b They have a lot of knowledge about how to stay healthy in hot weather.
  c They are used to living in very hot places.

5 In what way does the landscape of deserts sometimes cause problems?
  a It is difficult to drive on sand.
  b Everything looks the same, so it is difficult to find the right direction.
  c There are no other people around to offer help.

2 Match sentences 1–6 in the text with purposes a–f.

a giving advice ____
b describing a place ____
c making a comparison or contrast ____
d describing an event ____
e explaining a cause or result ____
f giving information or facts ____

3 Underline the subject in these sentences. Is it a noun (N) or a noun phrase (NP)?

1 Thunder crashed in the sky above us. ____
2 Homes that are built on cliff tops can collapse. ____
3 The ship's path was blocked by icebergs. ____
4 Steep wooded hills provide shelter for the deer. ____
5 For me, swimming is the perfect exercise. ____
6 Everyone in the room started yelling at him. ____

11C LANGUAGE

GRAMMAR: Third conditional

1 Choose the correct options to complete the sentences.

1. If you'd asked me, I _____ you.
   a would help   b would have helped
   c had helped
2. If they'd told us about the problem, Tom _____ it for them.
   a could have fixed   b could fix
   c had fixed
3. I would have called you if I _____ in trouble.
   a know you are   b knew you were
   c had known you were
4. If we'd taken the earlier flight, we _____ plenty of time.
   a would have   b would have had
   c have had
5. Lucy might have been upset if she _____ the truth about her boyfriend.
   a had known   b knew
   c knows
6. If I hadn't been sick, I would _____ to work.
   a go   b have gone
   c gone
7. I may not have been so angry if she _____ at me in front of everyone.
   a didn't yell   b doesn't yell
   c hadn't yelled
8. You wouldn't have had the accident if you _____ so careless!
   a hadn't been   b aren't
   c weren't

2 Complete the third conditional sentences with the verbs in parentheses in the correct order.

1. If Luis _____ attention, he _____ the instructions. (pay/understand)
2. I _____ a card if you _____ me it was her birthday. (send/tell)
3. Mira _____ earlier if she _____ the train. (take/arrive)
4. I _____ to the party if they _____ me. (invite/go)
5. If you _____ us, we _____ to the meeting. (not go/warn)
6. If it _____, the fair _____ a success. (not rain/be)
7. They _____ wet if they _____ umbrellas. (not get/take)
8. We _____ lost if you _____ to my directions! (listen/not be)

VOCABULARY: Extreme adjectives

3 Choose the correct adjectives to complete the sentences.

1. My friend Karina really makes me laugh – she's *starving / hilarious / miserable*.
2. She hated living on her own. It made her really *filthy / freezing / miserable*.
3. What a big car – it's *exhausted / enormous / hilarious*!
4. Turn the heat down – it's *freezing / boiling / furious*!
5. Our vacation couldn't have been better – it was *fantastic / furious / enormous*!
6. I was *hilarious / tiny / furious* because he'd been rude to me.

4 Complete the conversation with the correct adjectives.

Paulo So tell me about your vacation. Was it fun?
Yekta Yes and no. I hadn't realized how cold it would be at this time of year – it was ¹f_____! The hotel wasn't great, either. Our room looked so big on the website, but, actually, it was ²t_____. And it wasn't very clean. In fact, the bathroom was ³f_____. I had to ask them to clean it before I could use it.
Paulo What about the food? What was that like?
Yekta Well, it was OK, but there wasn't enough. Two hours after eating, we were both ⁴s_____!
Paulo And what about the town itself? Was that nice?
Yekta Yes, actually, it's full of beautiful old buildings, so it's really ⁵g_____. It's so incredible to look at. I have some great photos to show you.
Paulo Great! So did you spend most of your time looking around?
Yekta Yes, in fact, we walked so much on the first day, by the evening, we were both ⁶e_____.

PRONUNCIATION: Weak form of *have*

5 ▶ 11.2 Practice saying the sentences. Remember to pronounce the vowel sound in *have* as /əv/. Listen, check, and repeat.

1. If you'd gotten the bus, you wouldn't have been so late.
2. She would have paid less if she'd followed my advice.
3. He wouldn't have been so tired if he'd gone to bed earlier.
4. If I'd stayed longer, I might have seen Lily.
5. They might not have gotten lost if they'd listened to John.
6. She would have impressed me more if she hadn't been so rude!
7. If she'd taken some money, she could have bought some lunch.
8. If they'd listened to me, they wouldn't have made this mistake.

SKILLS 11D

SPEAKING: Making recommendations

1 ▶ 11.3 Mimi is talking about her travel plans with her friends Salma and Jack. Before you listen, try to complete the phrases they use for asking for ideas or making recommendations. Then listen and check.

1 Where _____ the best place to go?
2 Perhaps _____ get one of those round-the-world flights.
3 Do you have _____ about the best countries to visit?
4 I _____ going there in the monsoon season.
5 You _____ go to the Kiso Valley – it's gorgeous.
6 But if I _____, I'd keep my shoes and clothes near my bed.

2 ▶ 11.4 Read the conversation and complete 1–5 with a–e. Listen and check.

A I have 24 hours in New York on my way to Mexico. What do you think I should do while I'm there?
B You should definitely go on the Staten Island ferry.
A ¹____
B Yes it is, and you get great views of the Manhattan skyline.
A ²____
B If the weather's nice, I'd recommend getting a picnic from a deli.
A ³____
B You know, somewhere you can buy bread, sandwich meats, cheese, fruit, that sort of thing. There are plenty of delis in New York.
A ⁴____
B Yes, but only if the sun's shining! And of course, you really have to walk across Brooklyn Bridge.
A ⁵____
B A Broadway show, of course!

a So what you're saying is that I should buy some food and then find a park to eat it in.
b Oh, OK. It's free, isn't it?
c That sounds like fun. And what would you recommend doing in the evening?
d And where would be the best place to get lunch?
e I'm sorry. I'm not sure I've understood what you meant.

3 Complete the tag questions.

1 You can buy tickets in advance, _____?
2 The bus leaves from over there, _____?
3 It's the highest mountain in Latin America, _____?
4 You've been to Fiji, _____?
5 The weather won't be too bad, _____?
6 Clara recommended this hotel, _____?

4 Use your own words to summarize the advice given. The first one is done for you.

1 You can get a cheaper cab, but they're not always safe. You should always get an official one, even if you have to wait longer for it.
So what you're saying is that I need to get an official cab.

2 This restaurant is famous for its lamb dishes. The meat they use is all from local farms. I know you usually prefer seafood, but remember that we're a long way from the sea here, so it won't be very fresh.
So what you're saying is _____.

3 You can buy tickets at any of the tourist attractions. However, I'd recommend buying a tourist pass because then you can get into all the main museums, in addition to going on as many buses as you'd like, so it's really reasonable.
So what you're saying is _____.

11 REVIEW and PRACTICE

HOME BLOG **PODCASTS** ABOUT CONTACT

Tom and Sam talk about bad weather.

LISTENING

1 ▶ 11.5 Listen to the podcast and check (✓) the words that you hear.

a hurricane ____
b rainbow ____
c coast ____
d tornado ____
e sea ____
f hail ____
g monsoon ____
h flood ____
i storm ____

2 ▶ 11.5 Listen again. Complete the sentences with one or two words.

1 Bad weather is stopping a lot of tourists from going _____.
2 _____ once prevented Tom from leaving New York.
3 Isabella was staying in Florida when there was _____.
4 Isabella couldn't walk outside because it was so _____.
5 The people working in the hotel told the guests to stay _____.
6 Isabella thought _____ was like a monsoon.
7 When the hurricane finally stopped, Isabella had been in the hotel for _____.
8 Lots of _____ fell down because of the hurricane.

READING

1 Read Kate's blog on page 67 and number a–e in the order she mentions them (1–5).

a the features of a glacier ____
b a suggestion to the readers of the blog ____
c why she was worried about the helicopter flight ____
d an alternative to a heli-hike ____
e how they traveled to the glacier ____

2 Check (✓) the correct sentences.

1 Kate feels she just had a very special experience. ____
2 She is sure that she can describe how fantastic the experience was. ____
3 Before the helicopter flight, Kate had told Sophie that she was worried about it. ____
4 The helicopter flight was actually more comfortable than a plane flight. ____
5 The helicopter landed on the highest part of the glacier. ____
6 They stopped briefly before beginning the glacier walk. ____
7 The surface of the glacier was completely flat. ____
8 Heli-hikes only take place if the weather is good. ____

3 Find ten examples of extreme adjectives in the text.

REVIEW and PRACTICE 11

HOME **BLOG** PODCASTS ABOUT CONTACT

Guest blogger Kate writes about an amazing experience.

On top of the world

Yesterday, Sophie and I had the experience of a lifetime here in New Zealand – a day's "heli-hike" on the indescribably beautiful Franz Josef glacier. How can I possibly explain to you how spectacular it was? Since pictures sometimes speak louder than words, perhaps I'll start with a photo:

We arrived on the glacier after the most thrilling helicopter flight imaginable over the kind of landscape I'd only seen in nature shows: snow-capped mountain peaks and thick, dark forest. Beautiful! I'd been a little nervous about that helicopter flight. (Just ask Sophie!) An anxious flyer in the best of times, I'd had nightmares the previous night about falling out of the open door of the helicopter. In fact, after we had taken off (which was weird – that vertical lift!), it was no scarier than being on a normal plane. In fact it was probably a little smoother. And I had the incredible scenery to distract me. Twenty amazing minutes later, our helicopter landed at the bottom of two icefalls, which are like frozen waterfalls, and we all got out. After a ten-minute pause to admire the fantastic scenery, we started our three-hour glacier hike, led by the marvelous Daniel. (He was the perfect guide: friendly, full of interesting facts, and so much fun!) We hiked past enormous towers of ice (like something out of a fairy tale) and stood

on the edge of deep, seemingly bottomless holes, which Daniel told us are called *moulins*. And, best of all, we saw gorgeous, sparkling blue ice. (Yes, ice as blue as the sky!)

We arrived back at our hotel completely exhausted last night. Both of us were so tired that we slept for ten hours without waking up once. And this morning we were starving – our breakfast had never tasted so good!

As long as I live, I feel I'll remember this trip. We were incredibly lucky with the weather – nice and warm with sunny, cloudless skies. If the trip had been canceled because of bad weather, the tour company would have arranged for us to do a glacier valley walk, instead. I'm sure it would have been great, but nothing like this. To anyone considering a glacier hike at any point in their life, I say *just do it*. You won't regret it.

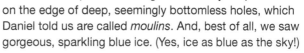

One of Sophie's. (Her camera's better than mine, and if I'm honest, so are her camera skills!)

UNIT 12 Getting away

12A LANGUAGE

GRAMMAR: So/Neither do I

1 Choose the best options to complete the replies.

1 I can eat a whole bag of that candy.
 a So can I.   b So do I.
 c So will I.
2 I'm not going to the concert.
 a Neither do I.   b So am I.
 c Neither am I.
3 I don't eat meat.
 a Neither am I.   b Neither do I.
 c So do I.
4 I don't like snow.
 a Really? I do.   b Really? I have.
 c Really? I didn't.
5 One day I'd love to travel the world.
 a So do I.   b So am I.
 c So would I.
6 I haven't seen Maria in ages.
 a Neither have I.   b So have I.
 c Neither do I.
7 We won't be able to go tonight.
 a Neither do I.   b Neither have I.
 c Neither will I.
8 I go to work on Saturdays.
 a So have I.   b So do I.
 c So am I.

2 Read the sentences and complete the replies.

1 A I've seen that movie twice.
 B So _____ I!
2 A I'm afraid I won't be free this weekend.
 B Neither _____ I.
3 A I don't like mornings.
 B Really? I _____. It's the best time of the day for me!
4 A James hates being late.
 B So _____ Ali.
5 A If I'm tired, I can sleep in till noon.
 B So _____ my brother.
6 A I don't trust that man.
 B Neither _____ I!
7 A I've never been to Italy.
 B Actually, neither _____ I.
8 A I'd love to live in Paris for a year.
 B So _____ I.
9 A I haven't spent any money this week.
 B Really? I _____! I bought a new phone yesterday.

VOCABULARY: Phrases with go and get

3 Match the meaning of get in sentences 1–10 with the verbs in a–e.

1 I'm getting really excited about our vacation. ____
2 Could you get me a book from the office, please? ____
3 Did you get my text this morning? ____
4 Great pants! Where did you get them? ____
5 We got to the airport an hour before our flight. ____
6 Jamie's just getting a blanket from the car. ____
7 I got a really nice rug from that new Swedish store. ____
8 It's getting cold, isn't it? ____
9 Have you ever gotten a prize in a competition? ____
10 She won't get to the concert on time tonight. ____

 a We received some complaints about the program.
 b Everyone became pretty angry about the situation.
 c We arrived at the station just before eight o'clock.
 d I always buy a few souvenirs while I'm on vacation.
 e Should I bring in dinner yet?

4 Complete the conversation with one word in each blank to complete the expressions.

Finn You ¹_____ away last month, didn't you, Anna?
Anna I did, yeah. I'm ²_____ away to college this September, so my parents thought we should all go ³_____ vacation before I leave home.
Finn So where did you go?
Anna We went to New Zealand. The first week we went scuba ⁴_____ north of Auckland. And we went ⁵_____ some beautiful walks in the mountains.
Finn Did you get to Wellington?
Anna Yeah, we ⁶_____ a trip to the south of the island the second week and took a guided ⁷_____ of Wellington. It was gorgeous. What about you? Have you ⁸_____ anywhere exciting this year?
Finn Nothing as good as that!

PRONUNCIATION: Auxiliary verbs and stress

5 ▶12.1 Read the sentences and replies. Underline the syllables in the replies that you think will be stressed. Listen, check, and repeat.

1 "Be careful!" "I will."
2 "I feel tired." "So do I."
3 "I don't know." "Neither do I."
4 "I passed the exam." "So did I."
5 "I've finished lunch." "I haven't."
6 "I have a cold." "So do I."

68

SKILLS 12B

LISTENING: Identifying agreement between speakers

1 ▶12.2 Listen to Neha and Lukas talking about vacations. Do they agree (A) or disagree (D) about 1–8?

	Agree	Disagree
1 Corsica is a beautiful island.		
2 It's nice to have very hot weather.		
3 It's best to go on vacation with other people.		
4 It's best to go on vacation with friends.		
5 Corsica has good hiking trails.		
6 Active vacations are better than lazy ones.		
7 Scuba diving is fun.		
8 Going on vacation is enjoyable.		

2 ▶12.2 Listen again. Are the following statements true (T), false (F), or not mentioned (N)?

1 Neha prefers the temperature to be over 30 degrees. ___
2 Neha is going on a hiking vacation. ___
3 Neha will be camping when she is in Nepal. ___
4 Lukas's friends, Karl and Trudi, work in Amsterdam. ___
5 The GR20 walk in Corsica is difficult. ___
6 Lukas enjoys spending days on the beach. ___
7 Lukas's friends usually get up very late on vaction. ___
8 Lukas's friends will go scuba diving with him. ___

3 ▶12.3 Look at the short sentences. Will the links marked _ be pronounced /w/ or /y/? Listen, check, and repeat.

1 He_always walks. ___
2 They_argue all the time. ___
3 It's so_interesting. ___
4 He's too_out of shape. ___
5 Why_are you laughing? ___
6 How_is Lucy? ___
7 We have a few_apples. ___
8 It's by_a lake. ___

4 Complete the words.

1 I like to walk around during the flight, so I'd prefer an a___ ___ ___ ___ seat.
2 You can ask a flight a___ ___ ___ ___ ___ ___ ___ for a glass of water.
3 Which g___ ___ ___ does our flight leave from?
4 You are only allowed one c___ ___ ___ ___-___ ___ b___ ___ on the flight.
5 Can you see our flight on the d___ ___ ___ ___ ___ ___ ___ board yet?
6 We went to the check-in desk and were given our b___ ___ ___ ___ ___ ___ ___ passes.
7 There are lots of stores and cafés in the d___ ___ ___ ___ ___ ___ l___ ___ ___ ___.
8 We have about half an hour before we l___ ___ ___ at JFK airport.
9 We had to take our shoes off when we went through s___ ___ ___ ___ ___ ___ ___.
10 The plane was unable to t___ ___ ___ o___ ___ because of bad weather.

12C LANGUAGE

GRAMMAR: Modals of deduction

1 Choose the correct options to complete the sentences or say if both are correct.

1. I keep seeing Miguel on Green Street. He _____ work near there.
   a can   b must
2. Of course, he _____ not even live here – he could just be visiting.
   a might   b may
3. I'm not sure if that's Gabriel's wife with him. It _____ be her.
   a could   b might
4. I can hear noises coming from the apartment, so someone definitely _____ be there.
   a must   b can
5. That girl is at least ten. Laura's daughter has just learned to walk, so it _____ be her.
   a can't   b might not
6. He looks exactly like Alfonso. It _____ be his twin brother.
   a can   b must
7. I thought he was French, but I guess I _____ be wrong.
   a could   b can
8. The woman in the photo is much younger than the man, so she _____ be his mother.
   a can't   b must

2 Complete the sentences with *must*, *might*, and *can't*.

1. When we met Jack, he was 80; that was years ago, so he _____ be very old by now.
2. I have no idea who that guy is. It _____ be Sofia's boyfriend because he's away.
3. I'm not sure if Rachel's here today. She _____ be.
4. Pedro's boss is bald. That man has loads of dark hair, so it _____ be him.
5. It's completely dark outside – it _____ be pretty late.
6. I don't know whether Alice is right about Carlos. She _____ be.
7. There's snow on the ground in the painting, so it _____ be winter.
8. You haven't eaten since breakfast. You _____ be hungry!

3 Complete the conversation with modal verbs. There may be more than one answer.

A Did I tell you I ran into Maria this morning?
B You did?
A Yeah, we talked for a little while. Do you think she's wealthy?
B She ¹_____ be. Apparently, she has three houses in London and two apartments in New York!
A But she looks young – she ²_____ be more than 30.
B I'm not sure. I think she ³_____ be 35.
A Anyway, I keep seeing her. Do you think she's working somewhere near by?
B I have no idea. I guess she ⁴_____ be – or she ⁵_____ be staying with her brother, Nico.
A Ah, I saw a woman who looked like Maria leaving a house on Elm Street yesterday. It ⁶_____ be her, then.
B It ⁷_____ be the same person – Nico has three sisters!

PRONUNCIATION: Sentence stress

4 ▶12.4 Underline the words that are stressed in these sentences. Listen, check and repeat.

1. She must be over twenty.
2. It can't be that late!
3. They might be stuck in traffic.
4. It could be her father, I suppose.
5. They must be on their way.
6. He can't be angry about it.
7. She might be listening to music.
8. They must be leaving.

SKILLS 12D

WRITING: Writing a review

Luxury Bicycle Trip in the Loire Valley, France

My friend and I went on this vacation last month. We had expected that a vacation with the word "luxury" in the title would provide fantastic hotels and good food.

Sadly, we were extremely disappointed. The hotels were pleasant enough, but very basic. In fact, at one of them, we even had to share a bathroom with the couple in the next room! In addition, the bikes they gave us were in very poor condition, and the maps were so out of date that we kept getting lost and having to use the GPS on my phone!

Luckily, the scenery was absolutely gorgeous, and we loved being out in the fresh air. Overall, I think this vacation would be good for students or young people who don't mind basic accommodations. However, it's not really suitable for anyone wanting a luxurious break.

Pizzeria Italia

Several of my friends had told me about the great pizzas at Pizzeria Italia. The pictures on the website looked really romantic, with candles and flowers, so I thought it would be perfect for a romantic evening with my girlfriend. Unfortunately, when we got there, we found almost the whole restaurant full of screaming kids! Someone had reserved most of the tables for an eight-year-old's birthday party. The noise was unbelievable, and it certainly wasn't romantic!

Also, we had expected everything to be freshly made. However, our pizzas were rather hard and difficult to chew. Clearly, the bases had come out of the freezer. The cheese was OK, but there was far too much of it – my girlfriend couldn't finish hers.

When we complained, we were told that the usual chef was off sick. They offered us a free meal on another night. I think children might enjoy it, and I wouldn't mind taking my nieces and nephews (especially if it's free!), but I'm pretty sure my girlfriend wouldn't want to come!

---

1 Read the two reviews by Tom Green. Are the statements true (T) or false (F)?

Luxury Bicycle Trip
1. He thought they would have high-quality hotels and food. _____
2. The hotels and food were as good as he had expected. _____
3. The bikes that they were given for the trip were good. _____
4. They were able to follow the maps easily. _____
5. They enjoyed the views of the countryside. _____
6. He thinks young people would enjoy the vacation. _____

Pizzeria Italia
7. Some of his friends had said that the pizzas were excellent. _____
8. He thought the restaurant would be noisy. _____
9. He enjoyed being with lots of children. _____
10. The pizzas were not as good as he had expected. _____
11. He thinks the restaurant is good for a romantic evening out. _____
12. He plans to take his girlfriend there again. _____

2 Complete the sentences with the adverbs of attitude in the box or your own ideas. There may be more than one answer.

> surprisingly   hopefully   unfortunately
> sadly   clearly   obviously   luckily

1. The waiters all seemed very stressed out. _____, the restaurant needs more staff.
2. It was a beautiful day when we visited the national park. _____, there weren't many people there.
3. A sign offered two meals for the price of one. _____, they were trying to attract more customers.
4. We were unable to ski today because of the bad weather. _____, it will be better tomorrow.
5. This place specializes in Japanese food, but, _____, they don't serve sushi or sashimi.
6. I came to this resort five years ago and loved it. _____, several large hotels have been built since then, which has changed its character.

3 Think of a place you have been to on vacation. Write a review.

- Before you start, make notes about what was good and bad about it.
- Say what you were hoping for before you went there.
- Say what it was really like.
- Say what kind of people it would be best for.

Include at least two adverbs of attitude.

12 REVIEW and PRACTICE

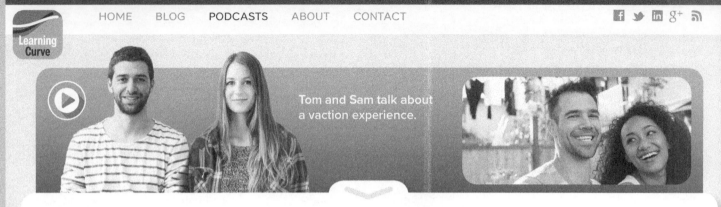

Tom and Sam talk about a vacation experience.

LISTENING

1 ▶ 12.5 Listen to the podcast and choose the correct options to complete the sentences.

1 Teresa likes going on vacation to places where
   a she can go hiking.
   b the countryside is beautiful.
   c there are fewer tourists.

2 While she was on vacation, Teresa met
   a a really interesting person.
   b someone that she knew from home.
   c the man who became her husband.

3 When Sam met someone she knew in Spain, they
   a went to the beach together.
   b had coffee together.
   c gave each other advice.

2 ▶ 12.5 Listen again. Are the statements true (T) or false (F)?

1 Teresa talks about a vacation in Spain. _____
2 Teresa saw someone she knew from home at the hotel. _____
3 The person she saw was a work colleague. _____
4 Teresa's husband did not believe that the person they had seen was Matthew. _____
5 Teresa and Matthew saw each other again during the vacation. _____
6 Sam enjoyed seeing someone she already knew on vacation. _____

READING

1 Read Simon's blog on page 73 and circle Y (Yes) if he says this or N (No) if he doesn't.

1 He never wants to travel by plane again. Y / N
2 He would be happier if people behaved differently in airports. Y / N
3 People get angry when he walks past them on the travelator. Y / N
4 He could not find anywhere to sit in Dulles airport. Y / N
5 People should not wear jewelry when traveling by plane. Y / N

2 Choose the correct options to complete the sentences.

1 Simon is irritated by
   a all aspects of traveling by plane.
   b passengers' behavior in the departure lounge.
   c passengers' behavior going through security.

2 Simon thinks people should
   a not look around them while they are on the travelator.
   b not use the travelator, but walk instead.
   c keep walking while they are on the travelator.

3 Simon says that in the departure lounge, he does not
   a sit in other people's seats.
   b sit next to people that he doesn't know.
   c put things on the seats next to him.

4 Simon says that some people do not realize that they
   a cannot take certain things in their luggage.
   b have to line up to go through security.
   c have to take off their clothes to go through security.

5 Simon says that people should
   a not forget to take their boarding passes.
   b keep their boarding passes safely in their hand luggage.
   c keep their boarding passes where they can quickly show them.

REVIEW and PRACTICE 12

HOME BLOG PODCASTS ABOUT CONTACT

Guest blogger Simon writes about his experience flying.

THE PAIN OF PLANES

I think I might be doing a bit too much flying at the moment. I seem to find the whole experience annoying, from check-in to customs. And here, in no particular order, is why:

The travelator – you know, the moving floor. OK, this thing is designed to get us quickly to our destination. But we can always help it along by *using our legs*. Why do so many people choose to stand on the thing and just look around them? It's not like the view's so great. And, more to the point, why do they look so annoyed when they have to move to one side to allow people like myself to walk past them? Well, I'm sorry, people, but I HAVE A PLANE TO CATCH!

OK, so I'm in the departure lounge, trying to calmly read my book in between nervously checking the departure board. Apparently, my fellow passengers don't like sitting next to complete strangers. Well, neither do I, but if I have to now and then, it's really not the end of the world. So I don't put my bags, coats, or cups of coffee on the seat next to me to stop people from using the seats FOR THE PURPOSE FOR WHICH THEY WERE INTENDED–which is what everyone else seems to do. In Dulles airport in Washington D.C. yesterday, for example, there were people standing around with *nowhere* to sit, for goodness' sake, while the seats to the left and right of me were piled high with hand luggage!

Now why, after *all these years*, do some people *still* attempt to go through security with bottles of liquid, sharp objects, etc? And then they look astonished when these items are removed by the officials. Come *on*, people – you must know it's against the law by now! Oh, and while we're on the topic of security, if you know you're going to have to remove an item of clothing or a piece of jewelry, just do it BEFORE you reach the front of the line. Because it REALLY SLOWS THINGS DOWN WHEN YOU DON'T.

Oh, and boarding passes ... don't get me started. You know you're going to have to show them to the flight attendant as you board the plane, so please have them *in your pocket*, and not buried somewhere in the bottom of your hand luggage!

Time to calm down! Think I'm going to go lie down in a darkened room for a while ...

WRITING PRACTICE

WRITING: Making a narrative interesting

I have a really good friend named Jon. We don't get together very often because he's a doctor, and he works very long hours. We usually keep in touch on social media, but one Thursday evening, just before I went to bed, I got a text message. It was Jon. He wanted to invite me to dinner "next Saturday." I replied to his text immediately and accepted his invitation. I was looking forward to seeing Jon because he's ¹_____ guy, and we have great conversations. He's also ²_____ – he always makes me laugh so hard.

On Saturday evening, I rode my bike over to his place. The weather was ³_____ – heavy rain and ⁴_____, and I couldn't wait to be in Jon's ⁵_____ living room. As soon as I arrived, I knew something was wrong. The windows of his house were dark, and when I rang the doorbell, nobody answered. I ⁶_____.

Jon was usually very reliable, so I thought that something bad had happened to him.

I got out my phone and texted him. There was no answer. There was nothing else I could do, so I decided to go home and wait until he replied. I spent most of the evening ⁷_____ checking my phone. After more than three hours, my phone rang. It was Jon. I ⁸_____ picked up my phone and asked him if he was all right. "Why did you think I wasn't OK?" he asked in a ⁹_____. "You invited me for dinner!" I said, a little ¹⁰_____ by now. Jon was ¹¹_____. "I invited you *next* Saturday, not *this* Saturday," he insisted.

Then we realized what the problem was. By "next Saturday" I thought he meant in two days, but what he really meant was in just over a week. We ¹²_____ with our plans in the future!

---

1 Read the blog post about a time when there was a communication problem and complete 1–12 with the words and phrases in the box.

> warm, cozy   terrible   eagerly   a really interesting   anxiously   amazed   puzzled voice
> have to be more careful   felt really worried   extremely amusing   very strong winds   annoyed

2 Which of 1–12 in exercise 1 match these features?

a descriptions of people ____ ____
b descriptions of places ____
c descriptions of the weather ____ ____
d descriptions of emotions and feelings
____ ____ ____ ____ ____ ____
e a comment on the events ____

3 <u>Underline</u> all the examples of *before, after, until,* and *as soon as* in the blog and read the sentences. Then choose the correct options to complete these sentences.

1 Please reply to this e-mail _____ you have finished reading it.
   a as soon as   b before   c until

2 Think very carefully _____ sharing photos on social media.
   a after   b until   c before

3 I won't know the time of the meeting _____ I get an e-mail from the organizer.
   a after   b until   c as soon as

4 _____ I had replied to Laura's text message, I realized I had given her the wrong number.
   a After   b Until   c Before

5 I kept in touch with Boris _____ 2010, when he moved abroad, and I lost his address.
   a after   b before   c until

6 I'll send you more information _____ I can go online.
   a until   b before   c as soon as

7 _____ our phone call, I invited her to my office so that we could speak face to face.
   a As soon as   b Until   c After

8 I need to make sure I know all the facts _____ I give my boss a call.
   a before   b as soon as   c after

4 Write a blog post about a time when there was a communication problem. Use the chart to plan some words and phrases to make your narrative interesting. Use different narrative tenses and time linkers.

descriptions of people, places, and events	
descriptions of emotions and feelings	
comments about the events	

WRITING PRACTICE

WRITING: Writing an informal e-mail

¹Dear Katie,

(A) ²It was a real pleasure to receive your e-mail. ³I apologize for taking so long to reply. I've been really busy, but I'm so pleased to hear that you've managed to make up with Amy. I know she's one of your closest friends, and it's horrible having a falling out with people.

(B) Did I tell you that I got on the college soccer team? ⁴It is very enjoyable, but we have to work extremely hard! We train twice a week, and there are games every weekend, all over the country. We even played in Montreal last month. It was an amazing trip! We won 3–0, and I scored two of the goals! I get along really well with all the other girls on the team. We have a lot of fun together – not just when we're playing soccer.

(C) So, are you still coming camping with us in August? I have a big tent if you want to share. I really hope you can come. ⁵I am very much looking forward to seeing you. Did I tell you that Don's coming as well? You two have a lot in common – he's a big rock fan, too, so at least you'll have something to talk about!

(D) By the way, did you hear about Jack? He's getting married! Apparently, his neighbor introduced him to her cousin and that was it – two months later, they were engaged. Incredible, isn't it?

(E) Speaking of marriage, how's your sister doing? Is her baby sleeping through the night yet? I'm definitely not going to have any children until I'm at least 35!

(F) Anyway, have to go – I have soccer training in half an hour. ⁶I look forward to hearing from you.

(G) ⁷Sincerely yours,

Emma

1 Read Emma's e-mail to her friend Katie. Emma's style is sometimes too formal. Rewrite the underlined phrases and sentences in a more informal style.

1 _____
2 _____
3 _____
4 _____
5 _____
6 _____
7 _____

2 Which paragraphs do the following things? Circle the words in the e-mail that show this.

1 change the subject   _____ _____
2 introduce a less important subject   _____
3 return to a subject   _____

3 Write an informal e-mail to one of your friends, telling him/her about a new friend you have made.

Include the following:
- an informal greeting
- some opening comments
- a paragraph about your new friend, e.g. how you met, your friend's personality, the things you have in common
- a paragraph in which you change the subject to ask your friend about someone you both know
- a paragraph about a less important subject
- a paragraph in which you return to the same subject as the previous paragraph
- a reason to end the e-mail
- an informal ending

Use informal discourse markers (*Anyway, So, By the way,* and *Speaking of*) to link the paragraphs.

WRITING PRACTICE

WRITING: Writing a cover letter

Dear Sir/Madam:

¹____ Senior Sales Representative, Electronic Goods, advertised in today's *Retail News*.

As you can see from my CV, ²____ and a certificate in soccer coaching. However, after working in the electronic goods department of a large store when I finished college, I decided that a career in sales would be more suited to my skills and personality.

After nine months at the department store, I got my current job as a sales representative with Secure Alarms, a company that provides security systems for businesses, as well as home owners. ³____, assessing their security needs, and making sales. To do this job, it is necessary to be highly organized and have excellent customer service skills.

⁴____ I am fascinated by sound systems, and keep up to date on all the latest products and developments. In addition, I have a good knowledge of cameras and photography, as well as smartphones and personal computers.

I am a very hardworking and reliable employee, and ⁵____. I would welcome the opportunity to work for a respected company like yours and, if my application is successful, I am confident that I would be a valuable addition to the team.

⁶____ and I look forward to hearing from you soon.

Sincerely,

Gillian Howes

1 Read Gillian's covering letter and match blanks 1–6 with phrases a–f.

a Thank you for considering my application,
b I am extremely interested in this position because
c I am responsible for meeting with customers
d I am writing to apply for the position of
e I have a degree in physical education
f I work very well as part of a team

2 Which of these things does Gillian do in her letter?

1 use formal language to end the main part of the letter ____
2 describe her personal qualities ____
3 ask about the salary ____
4 describe her qualifications ____
5 say why she would like the job ____
6 say she is good at languages ____
7 talk about her previous work experience ____
8 say which position she is applying for ____
9 explain her career goals ____
10 describe her attitude to work ____

3 Write a cover letter for this job. Remember to use formal language and include details of your qualifications, skills, and any relevant experience.

SALESCLERK, BJ OUTDOOR SPORTS

We are looking for smart, efficient sales staff for our new downtown store. The successful candidate will have:

- at least two years' experience working in a store
- excellent written and spoken English
- recognized proficiency in math
- a genuine interest in outdoor sports, especially climbing and skiing
- a knowledge of sports equipment

You will work as part of a large team. Our stores are always busy, so you must be able to work under pressure. To apply, please send your CV and a cover letter to Kelly Bagnold. Please provide details of your qualifications, skills, and any relevant experience.

WRITING: Writing a report

How to become an actor

(1) _____
Anyone can stand on a stage and say a few words, but if you really want to act, you need to learn how to do it correctly. Take acting classes if you can afford them, or consider going to drama school. In addition, you should read books on acting techniques. But above all, watch the actors you love!

(2) _____
Everyone has to start somewhere, so don't be shy. Look for any possible chance to act and grab it with both hands! Even taking part in a school play is good experience. I also suggest trying your local theater – they often need extras for their plays. This will give you experience on stage, as well as the chance to learn about other aspects of an actor's life, such as scenery, costumes, and lighting.

(3) _____
You may be a good actor, but if you can ride a horse, ski, play an instrument, or dance, as well, this could give you an advantage. Therefore, remember to include all your skills on your résumé, even if you don't think they are very relevant.

(4) _____
Make sure people know about you. An attractive personal website is very important. In addition to this, networking is essential. If you know a lot of people in the business, you are more likely to get work. If possible, I would also recommend getting an agent. Agents usually have a great number of contacts and can help you get parts in movies and plays.

(5) _____
It's not surprising that most actors give up within a year. If you fail to get jobs, it can damage your confidence. Moreover, you need to keep paying rent even if you're not working! But if you are really serious, continue trying and keep believing that you will find success. One day you will!

1 Read the report and match paragraphs 1–5 with headings a–h. There are three extra headings.

- a Study acting
- b Everyone can act
- c Start young
- d The importance of experience
- e Develop other skills
- f Write a great résumé
- g Tell people about yourself
- h Don't stop trying!

2 Complete the sentences with the verbs in the box in the correct form.

> include   get   talk   move   visit   keep

1 If you want a career in law, I suggest _____ to someone who already works as a lawyer.
2 Remember _____ your website up to date.
3 I recommend _____ several colleges before you decide on a progam.
4 For the best careers in finance, I suggest _____ to a big city, such as Hong Kong.
5 Before joining the army, I recommend _____ in the best shape that you can.
6 When you apply for a job, remember _____ an up-to-date résumé.

3 Complete these sentences with your own ideas.

1 Pilots must be physically healthy. In addition, _____.
2 To become a nurse, you will need good skills in maths and english, as well as _____.
3 Farmers need to be in shape and they have to be prepared to _____, as well.
4 Firefighters have to be prepared to work in dangerous situations. Moreover, _____.
5 If you own your own café, you often have to work very long hours. In addition to this, _____.
6 If you want to be an author, you should read as much as you can! In addition, _____.

4 Think of a job that you would like to do. Write a report on the best way to get that job. Use ideas from exercises 2 and 3 to help you.

- Plan four or five section headings.
- Include factual information.
- Make recommendations using *suggest*, *recommend*, and *remember*.

WRITING PRACTICE

WRITING: For-and-against essays

In 2016, France became the first country to make it illegal for supermarkets to throw away unsold food. Should all countries do the same?

(A) _____ Some of them even put substances in their garbage bins so that the food cannot be eaten, even if it is still in good condition. This is to stop people from taking the food out of the bins. Many people believe that this is wrong, and that all countries should do the same as France. They should make supermarkets give their unsold food to charities so that they can give it to the poor people in our society who really need it.

(B) _____ After all, if supermarkets can't sell this food, it is better for charities to use it to feed the poor. Also, if a supermarket gives its unsold food to a charity, the people who work for the charity can make sure it is safe to eat. However, if people take food out of the garbage bins themselves, it could be dangerous to eat, and it might make them sick.

(C) _____ The supermarkets have paid for the food, so they should be able to decide what to do with it. In addition, if supermarkets had to pack the food up in a special way to give it to the charities, it would increase their costs. As a result, supermarkets would probably raise their prices, so it would be more expensive for the rest of us to do our shopping.

(D) _____ Although I think that the French made this law for good reasons, in my view, it would be better to allow supermarkets to decide for themselves what to do with their unsold food.

1 Read the essay and match paragraphs A–D with topic sentences 1–5. There is one extra topic sentence.

1 On the one hand, this may seem like a good idea.
2 Supermarkets often throw away large amounts of food waste.
3 To sum up, I do not believe that all countries should do the same as France.
4 Supermarkets are businesses, and they cannot afford to give people free food.
5 On the other hand, is it right for the government to interfere in business in this way?

2 Which of these arguments does the writer use?

1 **For**
  a We should help people who are hungry.
  b It is better to give unsold food to people who can use it.
  c It is a waste of money to throw away good food.
  d Businesses should do something to help poor people.
  e Food waste is bad for the environment.

2 **Against**
  a Giving food to charities requires extra work for supermarkets and may increase prices.
  b Supermarkets should use better systems to reduce food waste.
  c We should give poor people the food they need – not just the food nobody else wants.
  d This system would encourage people not to work.
  e Supermarkets should be free to do what they like with the food that belongs to them.

3 Complete these topic sentences for the essay with ideas from exercise 2 or your own ideas.

1 The main advantage of _____
2 However, one disadvantage _____
3 On the one hand, _____
4 On the other hand, _____
5 To sum up, _____

4 Rewrite the final three paragraphs of the essay above and reach a different conclusion.

- Use at least one new argument for and one new argument against.
- Start each paragraph with a topic sentence and a linking phrase.
- Remember to use formal language.

WRITING PRACTICE

WRITING: Writing a review

ACTIVITY VACATION IN FRANCE

I went on this vacation with a group of friends. According to the website, it was going to be the adventure of a lifetime in one of the most gorgeous parts of France, surrounded by fantastic mountain scenery. In fact, in the end, it wasn't really an adventure vacation at all.

On Day One, we were supposed to go white water rafting in a huge canyon. Sadly, because of a storm the night before, the water was too dangerous, and we ended up going for a short walk, instead. On Day Three, the plan was to go skiing on a nearby glacier, where there's snow all year round. However, our driver clearly didn't know the way, and it took us so long to get there that we only had an hour for skiing by the time we finally reached the glacier.

This vacation should have been perfect for a group of young people like us, but, actually, it was a big disappointment. I wouldn't recommend it to anyone.

HIKING IN NEPAL

My brother and I went hiking in Nepal in the summer. It was something I had always wanted to do. Obviously, I had expected it to be tough, but I don't think I realized just how exhausted I would be at the end of each day! However, I improved quickly, and by Day Four, I was feeling in much better shape and was really enjoying the experience. By the end of the vacation, I didn't want to stop walking!

The vacation brochure had warned us that the food wouldn't be of restaurant quality because everything had to be carried. Surprisingly, it was actually pretty good. We were always hungry from walking, and the meals were both tasty and large!

This vacation is perfect for anyone looking for a real adventure. But I would recommend getting in better shape than I was before you go, and it wouldn't be suitable for anyone with health problems.

1 Read the two reviews and match 1–6 with what the reviewers say (a–j).

1 expectations of the vacation in France ____ ____
2 expectations of the vacation in Nepal ____ ____
3 what the vacation in France was really like ____ ____
4 what the vacation in Nepal was really like ____ ____
5 who would enjoy the vacation in France ____
6 who would enjoy the vacation in Nepal ____

a very adventurous
b no one
c problems with the activities
d physically hard
e rather boring
f extremely tiring
g good food
h people that are in good shape and healthy
i simple food
j beautiful scenery

2 Complete the sentences with your own ideas for vacation reviews.

1 Our plane was delayed, and we didn't land until after midnight. Luckily, _____.
2 We had expected to have a view of the beach. Unfortunately, _____.
3 I thought a vacation in Japan would be extremely expensive. Surprisingly, _____.
4 The hotel room was cold and dirty. Obviously, _____.
5 We weren't able to visit the rainforest because of the hurricane. Hopefully, _____.
6 The website showed pictures of happy families playing in the sun. Sadly, _____.
7 It wouldn't have been safe to go into the jungle alone. Clearly, _____.

3 Write a review of a visit to somewhere with beautiful or interesting scenery.
Before you start, write down ideas for things you will say were good or bad. Remember to include the following:

• what your expectations were before you went
• what it was really like
• who would or wouldn't enjoy the experience
• at least two adverbs of attitude (*unfortunately, hopefully,* etc.)

Richmond
58 St Aldates
Oxford
OX1 1ST
United Kingdom

Printed in Brasil
ISBN: 978-84-668-2844-4

© Richmond / Santillana Global S.L. 2017
Reprinted, 2025

Publishing Director: Deborah Tricker
Publisher: Luke Baxter
Editors: Fiona Hunt, Helen Wendholt
Americanizer: Deborah Goldblatt
Proofreaders: Tas Cooper, Shannon Neill
Design Manager: Lorna Heaslip
Cover Design: Richmond
Design & Layout: Lorna Heaslip, Oliver Hutton, Colart Design
Photo Researcher: Magdalena Mayo
Audio production: TEFL Audio

Photos:
Prats i Camps; ALAMY/Photo 12, Sylvie Bouchard, Dinendra Haria, Peter Wheeler, age fotostock, travelstock44, Dave Stevenson, Moviestore collection Ltd, Jim West, Mikael Damkier, Nathaniel Noir, PURPLE MARBLES, Matthew Chattle, jaileybug, ONOKY - Photononstop, Newscast Online Limited, PJF Military Collection, Kerry Dunstone, FORGET Patrick/SAGAPHOTO.COM, Chuck Pefley; GETTY IMAGES SALES SPAIN/Thinkstock; ISTOCKPHOTO/Getty Images Sales Spain; ARCHIVO SANTILLANA

Cover Photo: iStockphoto/Getty Images Sales Spain

Impressão e acabamento: Meta Brasil
Lote: 802791
Cód: 290528444

All rights reserved. No part of this book may be reproduced, stored in a retrieval system or transmitted in any form by any means, electronic, mechanical, photocopying, recording or otherwise, without the prior permission in writing of the Publisher.

We would like to thank the following reviewers for their valuable feedback which has made Personal Best possible. We extend our thanks to the many teachers and students not mentioned here.
Brad Bawtinheimer, Manuel Hidalgo, Paulo Dantas, Diana Bermúdez, Laura Gutiérrez, Hardy Griffin, Angi Conti, Christopher Morabito, Hande Kokce, Jorge Lobato, Leonardo Mercato, Mercilinda Ortiz, Wendy López

The Publisher has made every effort to trace the owner of copyright material; however, the Publisher will correct any involuntary omission at the earliest opportunity.